Introduction
Who is Jimmy Reed

Jimmy Reed has an extensive background in the field of Real Estate Investing having bought, sold and managed over 300 units all by the age of thirty. Jimmy began his investment career in the late 1980's while still working full time. As he developed a solid understanding of real estate investing, Jimmy went on to specialize in the areas of Wholesaling, Probate, Owner Financing, Notes, and Cash Flow Rentals along with other investment strategies.

After several years of success in Real Estate Investing as well as teaching workshops and mentoring other investors in the Dallas / Fort Worth area, a National Real Estate Consultant with one of the country's top training organizations approached Jimmy to help create their training programs for their students. He was instrumental in creating their Mentoring, Wholesale and Probate programs. These "trainings" put Jimmy in some of the hottest markets in the country such as Hawaii, New York, Cozumel, Panama and even Costa Rica.

Today, Jimmy brings you *No Fear Real Estate*. In this book, he discusses how to remove the fear from lack of knowledge that is holding you back, and discusses how to ●Wholesale real estate via Assignments and Double Closings ● Find great deals via Probate ● Buy, Rent, and Hold for long term wealth ● Sell properties with Owner Financing ● Create Notes, and how to hold those notes or sell them ● Use other people's money instead of your own● Become wealthy by using IRA's to do all your buying & selling and then receiving the profits back tax free or tax deferred. All of these strategies will provide you with the tools you need to start building your real estate portfolio and take you to a new level of achievement!

Currently, Jimmy is the founder of Real Estate Equity Development, Inc. and other companies which specialize in the buying & selling of real estate, and providing reality based information & trainings for others who want to learn about the exciting opportunities in real estate, and how to create residual income through rental properties. Along with creating the "Fast Track to Wholesaling" Training Camp he is also co-author of "The Hidden Treasures and Profits of Probate" Training. And he is the founder of www.1REclub.com , the Premier Real Estate Club located in Fort Worth, TX.

Copyright © 1991 – 2010 by

Reed Investment Property's

Revised © 2002, 20018 by

Real Estate Equity Development   www.JimmyReed.net

All Rights Reserved

P.O. Box 122654

Fort Worth, TX 76121

Forward by Bill Barnett

Congratulations, you've just bought a great book from one of the few trainer/investors I know that's been doing this longer than I have.

I meet Jimmy Reed some twenty plus years ago and he was already a seasoned pro.
I've had the pleasure of being his friend and learning from him that entire time.

In Jimmy's latest book, No Fear Real Estate you'll find a treasure trove of investing knowledge. As a well-rounded investor you don't want to be cornered by using one strategy for your business. In No Fear Real Estate you'll find a profit plethora of strategies that include:

Wholesale
Probate
Rehab
Subject To
Single Family Rentals
Multi-Family
And Much, Much More!

One of the few people I talk to about deals where I'm seeking their input, that's my friend and colleague, Jimmy Reed...Read, Enjoy, Learn and Profit!

Thanks Jimmy,

G. William Barnett II (Bill)
National Best Selling Author of "Are You DUMB Enough to be RICH?"
Nationally Syndicated radio host of "Real Estate NOW! With Bill Barnett"

TABLE OF CONTENTS

Introduction..Page 1

Forward ....Page 2

Part I   Making Money in Real Estate

Chapter 1: How Can I Make Money in Real Estate? ....Page 4

Chapter 2: How Is Money Made in Specific Market? ....Page 12

Chapter 3: What Makes a Deal Good?...Page 18

Part II Making Money with No Money

Chapter 4: Purchasing a Property – Contracts – Offer to Purchase ....Page 21

Chapter 5: Motivated Sellers – The Key to Great Deals..........................Page 23

Chapter 6: What Do You Do When You Get a Deal?..................................Page 28

Part III   Choosing Your Exit Strategies

Chapter 7: Wholesale..Page 30

Chapter 8: Buy, Fix, and Sell..Page 33

Chapter 9: Buy, Fix, and Hold...Page 38

Part IV   Getting Started

Chapter 10: What Next?..Page 46

Chapter 11: Beginning Investors' Most Frequently Asked Question. ....Page 51

Glossary ....Page 58

Making Money in Real Estate

How Can I Make Money in Real Estate

Through the years, one of the most frequently asked questions I get is, "How can I make money in real estate?" I always answer, "Multiple ways: appreciation, cash flow, tax benefits, and most of all, equity at the time of purchase."

1. Characteristics of a Successful Investor

Mindset

The very first thing you must have to be a successful real estate investor is the proper attitude and motivation to be an entrepreneur. If your mind is not focused on success; if you don't have the willingness and patience to do the work it takes to succeed, then you're going to be easily discouraged.

As I have trained students over the years, I always get them used to saying the word **"Easy."** In our **one-day, two-day, three-day live trainings, on-line trainings and mentoring sessions**, the students are encouraged to use the word "easy." It helps with their motivation and confidence, and soon they actually believe what I am teaching them is easy, because it really *is* easy!

Work Ethic

A true entrepreneur also realizes that failure is not defeat; it is a part of learning. It's a matter of failing forward, learning from mistakes, and knowing that "luck" is what happens when hard work and opportunity meet. The truly successful person is the one who falls, but gets up, learns from the fall, and keeps going.

Financial Situation

The strategies you use in real estate are determined by whether or not you have cash available. Investing in real estate can be done either way, with or without cash, but you must know up front what you realistically have to work with. Your exit strategies are determined in the beginning based on your current financial situation. Do you have cash? Or are you dead broke?

How is Money Made in Real Estate?

Equity

The best way to make money in real estate is to have equity. I am an old school investor: I make money when I buy. I *always* purchase properties that have equity in them. This is due mostly to my investing experience in north Texas. We do not get as much appreciation here as has been historically seen in other areas of the nation, such as California and New York. Therefore, I have always purchased my appreciation.

Motivated Sellers

Let's talk about ways to make money in any market, even if you're dead broke. It all starts with a Motivated Seller. As investors, we are looking for deals. These are not generally found in the "pretty" properties listed for sale on Zillow, Trulia, major real estate brokerage websites or the MLS (Multiple Listing Service). They are mostly found in distressed properties that may need TLC. These may be properties vacant due to foreclosure, probate, or other situations where you as investor become the problem-solver. Distressed conditions cause stressed owners, who may in turn become motivated sellers. Even if the seller is motivated, it must be a *deal for an investor*: there has to be enough equity in the property for immediate profit potential. Distressed properties tend to ensure equity coupled with motivation. Focusing on these types of properties provides a great starting point for your journey in real estate investing. Even properties with little to no current equity can still be profitable with the correct exit strategies in place.

Three main ways to invest in real estate

Wholesale – "controlling real estate"

The first thing for you to understand about making money in real estate is that we can do it without actually buying property. I like to use the phrase, "controlling real estate." We actually control the property via purchase contracts, letters of intent and double closing. To control a piece of property that has equity, we put it under contract for a period of time subject to some kind of escape clause. During this time, we seek out investors in our markets who need deals, can close quickly, and have cash. This technique is usually known as wholesaling.

Wholesaling allows us to control a piece of real estate via a purchase contract. Once we have a contract with a motivated seller for a piece of property, we quickly turn around and find a cash buyer to sell our contract to via an assignment contract. The assignment contract is for more than our original purchase price. Hence, we are assigning our contract, our right to purchase the property, to another buyer for a fee. This is how I got started back in the '80s, and it is still my favorite exit strategy today, mostly because it requires little to no money out of my own pocket.

Some investors have the ability to buy a property by getting a loan, partnering with someone else who has cash, forming a joint venture or syndication, or even using a self-directed IRA to fund the purchase. If these options are open to you, you have additional exit strategies available. Actually buying the property – putting it under contract and then closing on it – puts you in a holding position, whether short or long term.

Buy, Fix & Sell – "rehab or flip"

One exit strategy for a short-term holding position is Buy, Fix and Sell. More than likely, you had to get financing and are now faced with repairing and updating the property, better known as "rehabbing." Rehabbing has the most profit potential for investors who buy the property at the right price (i.e. with lots of equity). However, that equity can be quickly eaten up if you don't know how to control rehab costs. If you have never rehabbed a property, I do not suggest this route starting out. Some new investors start this way because they have watched some DIY or HGTV television show about "flipping" properties. They believe they can do it because it only took 30 minutes to do the same thing on some episode they watched.

In real life, rehabbing is work. You must be able to oversee the job, deal with contractors, building codes, permits and inspections, as well as finance the repairs. Make sure you have the problem of access to necessary funds solved in the beginning while considering the purchase. The *stumbling block* I see among new investors *is not factoring in* enough money for the repairs at the beginning when structuring the deal, and then ending up overpaying later for the repairs on the property. One way to avoid this problem is to network with and learn from seasoned investors who have experience rehabbing properties. A great place to do this is at local real estate clubs. The best thing about these is that you can find deals there as well as people who will buy them, fund them and repair them! I call it "One Stop Shopping."

Once you become an experienced investor and have a great team to work with, then the Buy, Fix and Sell strategy is one of the best ways to make a large profit in one-to-four family units. Please note that I did not say multi-family here. I have owned plenty of apartment complexes in my time, and there is a reason why they're called "complex." They should only be attempted by a seasoned investor. New investors should start with single family properties. The techniques we will focus on in this book, once learned and mastered, can also be used on other types of properties. However, if you like taking arrows in the *ass*ets, then go ahead; dive straight into those larger properties first and have fun!

Buy, Fix & Hold – "landlord"
One of the most popular long-term investment strategies in real estate is Buy, Fix and Hold. This opens the doors to several opportunities, one of which is cash flow. With enough rental properties and a positive cash flow for each one of them, you could soon replace your monthly paycheck while building your real estate empire. You also start creating equity through appreciation. This gives you the ability to tap the equity later on to do more deals and, in some cases, do them tax free. Make sure you have a good, experienced real estate CPA as part of your team. Let him guide you in situations that relate to tax-free or self-dealing when it comes to refinancing and IRAs.

This is the path to creating wealth. Imagine owning ten houses, one purchased every year for ten years, each with a value of $100,000. If you eventually let the rents generated pay the mortgage, over time you would own the property free and clear as long as you did not tap the equity. Once you own them all free and clear, you have a net worth of one million dollars. Not bad for one house a year over a ten year period.

But before you get all excited, let me give you the last part of Buy, Fix and Hold. You still have to get the property fixed up in order to rent it. This means you are most likely going to have to do some rehab work, dealing with those issues mentioned above.

The one aspect of Buy, Fix and Hold that can either make or break you is property management. It is in your best interest to hire the very best professional property manager available – they are well worth the cost. If you focus on hiring someone affordable, you may end up soon having the desire to get out of real estate. If you attempt management on your own, you may still find yourself wanting to quit real estate altogether. If you can't afford the best, or you don't have a great property manager on your team, then learn to be a great property manager yourself. No one will ever have more of a vested interest in your property than you.

Understanding the Market
The first thing you must realize is that the real estate market operates in cycles. It goes up and down, just like a roller coaster. Some rises and falls are gentle and others will either terrify or exhilarate you!

Seller's Market
When the market is headed up the hill, this is what is typically called a seller's market. This means there are more buyers than there are available properties. You may see multiple offers on the same property. The Sellers can be picky about financing and terms of the contracts because they have several contracts to choose from. Buyers become motivated because the interest rates may be low, and they can get a good price for their current home, so they see it as a good time to make a move. However, when they start getting frustrated because they're losing out in multiple offer situations, they will start offering to pay over list price as well as for lots of things that the seller usually pays for – title costs, realtor fees, and any difference between appraised value and negotiated sales price.

This does not mean that sellers can get away with no repairs – there are certain major components (electrical, plumbing, structural) that must pass appraisal for the buyer's lender to approve a loan. While these motivated buyers may be offering to pay over appraisal, and bring difference to the closing table of the appraisal price doesn't meet the negotiated sales price, they still need the property in "move-in ready" condition. On the other hand, if the seller is not getting other offers and the property still meets your criteria, it may still qualify as a good investment for your buy and hold portfolio, with potentially great cash flow. The key here will be to buy it for the right price – and not become a motivated buyer. These criteria and ROI (return-on-investment) strategies are also covered more in-depth during our trainings.

Buyer's Market
When the market is headed down the big roller coaster dip, something happens; it becomes what we call a buyer's market. This is what you wait your whole life for as an investor. It means

there are very few people in the market to buy real estate, so sellers cannot get rid of their properties. In order to stay competitive, they must lower the price on the properties. Since the market is bad to begin with, and there may already be an influx of properties in foreclosure arriving on the market daily, the seller is forced to reduce the price even more. If the seller's property is in need of repair, then they know that they must either make the repairs themselves or discount the price even more.

Buyers have a choice of good deals in this type of market, so the sellers must make their properties attractive in order to sell them. To an investor, this means price! Keep in mind it is also a great time for homeowners to buy, but they don't. They are usually scared not only because of the market conditions, but also because banks tighten up their loan approval requirements. As a result of that fear, very few homeowners take advantage of the opportunity to pick up a deal. Instead, investors are just about the only buyers available to the sellers in this market. And even then, many investors shy away from doing anything because of fear or lack of knowledge.

Timing

In keeping with the roller coaster analogy of the real estate market, take a look at this historic graph of home values, based on the work by Yale Economist and Nobel Prize winner Robert Schiller.

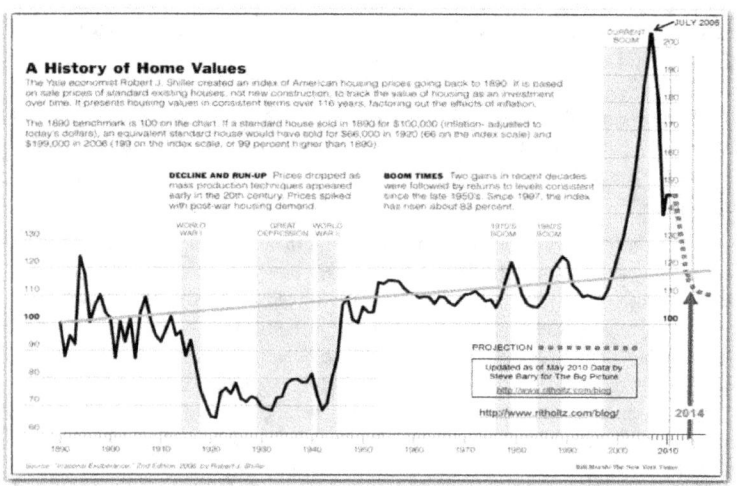

Mr. Schiller provides us the ability to see what makes a good deal: timing! We must always keep in mind that timing in real estate is crucial for optimal returns.

Where a downturn in the real estate market may cause fear and panic in the average homeowner or investor, the savvy investor knows it's a time of incredible opportunity. Smart investors know that real estate is always one of the safest investments if bought at the right price, in the right location, during the perfect economic downturn. There is opportunity here: when others are fearful is the perfect time for us to buy. Hardly anyone else is interested in buying real estate at this time, so the low levels of competition enable us to get the best prices. This is when millionaires are made.

This fear is what creates good deals in real estate. We just need to know that our exit strategies are not going to be the same as the average investors', so we don't worry about the same things they do. Their fear allows us to step in for a period of time and snatch up some great deals while their lack of knowledge scares them into missing out.

One of my favorite movies is *A Wonderful Life*. In the movie, there is a scene about the Great Depression. The taxi driver tells George Bailey that it looks like a run on his bank, the Bailey Building & Loan. It is, and everyone is willing to sell their shares to mean old Mr. Potter at a discount for cash immediately. George convinces many of his shareholders not to do it. He tells them, "Potter wants you to be scared; its how he makes his money." Later in the movie when George goes and sees Mr. Potter, they have a conversation about the time George saved the Bailey Building & Loan, and Potter saved everything else. Mr. Potter says that he and George were the only ones that kept their heads while everyone else was panicking.

When you look at Shiller's graph, you can actually see in history when that run on the bank occurred. In fact, you can see all of the market down times we've had in this country since 1890. Now look at what happened after each downturn in the market; it always came back up. For over one hundred and ten years, it has been tracked. It really is like riding a roller coaster when it comes to investing in real estate; the market always goes up and always comes down. Time it right, and you could be very wealthy the next time the roller coaster goes back up. Before we move on, think about where the market is for you right now?

Keep this graph on your desk where you can see it. Every time you sense fear creeping up on you, just remember what George Bailey did: he kept his cool and stood firm. Oh, and Mr. Potter? Well, he got richer, but not necessarily any happier!

You know, I watch that movie every Christmas Eve with my family, and it's a great classic. However, it's not about getting rich, nor is that why I like it so much. Watch it, and you will see it's a great reminder that if you treat folks right, help them out when they have problems, have some Faith in what you were put here to accomplish, and do what pleases God, you really can have a Wonderful Life.

Another mark of fear in the real estate market, and an early indicator of a downturn, is a trend change in the number of realtors. The graph below shows what happens when fear sets in:

Realtors start to get out of the business during a market downturn because they focus on homebuyers for their sales. When there's not enough buyers to keep the realtors in business, many who were only barely getting by in a good market have little to no business in a down market, and will find other lines of work.

Something else to watch for is how the country reacts to fear in the market. Many high-end markets, which tend to have more foreclosures, start to drop in sales. In fact, median markets seem to ride out the downturns of the real estate cycle much better because of the lower price points of property. The average prices in these markets make them favorable places to buy homes. The homeowner can buy more house for less money. As an investor, you might even start to consider going outside of your home market to find deals. If you do, you need a team in that market that can help you understand what you need in order to do business there. You also want to contact other investors in those areas whom you may be able to work with and extend your network. On the next page is a graph that will help you see the increase in prices by county across the nation. Tip: the green states are where you can make some serious green stuff: CASH!

The Counties in which Home Prices are Rising

Change in House Price Index by County
(From Q4 2006 to Q4 2007)

Percent Change in House Price Index
- Greater than 5.47% increase
- 4.171% to 5.47% increase
- 1.75% to 4.17% increase
- Less than 1.75% increase
- Any decrease or no change

Source: House Price Index from the Office of Federal Housing Enterprise Oversight

Now this graph is a bit old, but you can see the concept I am talking about. As the market changes, there will be times that other markets will have more profit opportunity than your home market. As a matter of fact, I actually invest outside of the U.S.A., in markets such as Panama and Costa Rica, because of great returns. Fear is definitely something we had to overcome in order to invest there, so I don't want to hear you whining about "well, it's two states away from where I live." I actually wrote on article in 2008 on this titled, "Leap Over to a New Country." If you join my network on my website, www.JimmyReed.net, I will send you a copy for FREE! Oh, and for right now, joining my network is FREE, too!

How is Money Made in Specific Markets?

Up Market

Buy & hold rentals – strong cash flow

Buying & selling real estate notes – still many performing & non-performing notes that have better cash flow than actual rental properties

Focus is more on probate to find investment properties. Also look outside your own "backyard" market – not the same market from city to city or state to state

Also see more on this on Page 15 Changing Markets

Down Market

In 2008, we were faced with an extremely large number of foreclosed properties in the United States. We had recently switched administrations in Washington, D.C., and there was a lack of investor confidence. This lack of confidence, and even downright fear, coupled with the collapse of the housing "bubble" due, in part, to a high percentage of non-performing sub-prime mortgages, crippled the real estate industry.

Opportunity

Most would say that you should stay away from real estate in this situation. What you need to know is that it is precisely this economic condition that creates opportunities, and as I tell my students in all my trainings, "Opportunity only lasts five minutes!" Most will focus on fear when they should be shouting, "OH, YEAH! Opportunity!" There is a great scripture that refers to this: **2 Timothy 1:7 (NLT) "For God has not given us a spirit of fear and timidity, but of power, love, and self-discipline."**

Just as when riding a roller coaster, the fun part to the investor is not going up the big hill because that's when everyone wants to get in and start investing. This big hill, going up the peak of the real estate market, is also known as a seller's market. There is more demand than supply, resulting in multiple buyers vying for the same properties, driving up prices, and even paying over appraisal prices.

The fun part for an investor is going down the hill; which is what we call a buyer's market. Buyers have a choice of good deals in this type market, so the sellers must make their properties attractive in order to sell them. To an investor, this means price! Keep in mind it is also a great time for homeowners to buy, but they don't. They are usually scared not only because of the market conditions, but also due to banks tightening up their loan approval requirements. As a result of their back seat of the roller coaster mentality, very few homeowners take advantage of the opportunity to pick up a deal. Instead, investors are just about the only buyers available to the sellers in this market. And even then, many investors shy away from doing anything because of fear or lack of knowledge.

As we start to go down the tracks of this falling market, we keep our eyes peeled for increasing numbers of foreclosures, banks fearing to lend money, and still increasing rents. This is what you wait your whole life for as an investor. It means there are very few people in the market to buy real estate, so sellers cannot get rid of their properties. In order to stay competitive, they must lower the price on the properties. Since the market is bad to begin with, and there is already an influx of properties in foreclosure arriving on the market daily, the seller is forced to reduce the price even more. If the seller's property is in need of repair, then they know that they must either make the repairs themselves or discount the price even more.

When the market hits its lowest points, everyone calls it a crash. This is a very recognizable time because everyone is jumping out of real estate. What you need to know is that now is the time to pick up properties, which could be as much as 30%, 40%, 50% or more below market value.

Be careful, because at this point everyone will tell you to dump your inventory and get out of real estate; or that you're crazy to even think about investing in such a market. These investors are only interested in riding the coaster up the hill; which is precisely when most people want to invest and actually end up losing money in the long run. They have speculated that the coaster will just keep going up. This ideology is more gambling than investing, because smart investors know that there are always both peaks and valleys in any type of market. One of my favorite scriptures is **Hosea 4:6, "My people are destroyed from lack of knowledge."** Folks, as investors, we must always remember that real estate changes and business changes. If we do not keep up with the trends and obtain the knowledge we need to succeed, then we will be destroyed in our business and our life. We must always keep learning in life!

I suggest you focus on the fun part; as we near the bottom of the big drop is when we jump on the ride. From a seasoned investor's viewpoint, we want to sit in the front seat of the first car of that roller coaster so we can watch where we're headed. By being in the first car over the hill, we can get a good idea of how far down the plunge goes. I'm not saying we can see exactly how far down the track goes, but we can watch its direction.

Buying Equity

As we start obtaining these undervalued properties, we are automatically buying equity. It may not have a large amount of equity at the time of purchase, but it will be future equity once the market heads back up again. This is what we talked about earlier as one of the best ways to make money in real estate. Keep in mind, sellers now become more motivated. This, coupled with no demand from buyers, helps us to buy properties far enough below value that we actually begin adding real estate equity into our portfolio. Also remember that as properties go into foreclosure, homeowners abandon them, leaving them subject to deterioration from vandalism and lack of maintenance. These distressed properties, along with distressed owners and a troubled market, spell opportunity for us as real estate investors.

Don't worry; most of you are thinking right now, "Even if we get a good deal, who are we going to sell it to?" Well, that's easy. Every cycle of real estate, every up and down, creates a unique group of buyers. Homeowners we sell to in up markets tend to have good credit and can get loans. Homeowners we sell to in down markets tend to have bad credit, yet they usually have cash. This opens up the opportunities to sell properties in a down market using owner financing, lease options and rent-to-own strategies. As a real estate investor, you are now and forevermore a problem solver.

High Demand for Rentals

Different markets create different demands for rentals. In a down market, some potential tenants will be those who have recently lost their home to foreclosure. Of these, several may still have their jobs, but have had other life circumstances (illness, taking care of elderly parent, children's student loans) that have forced them to sell their homes. These additional, unexpected costs, combined with rising taxes and insurance, created higher payments than they could afford. Keep in mind that some of these people paid over appraisal price for their homes in a hot seller's market, and were upside down in the property when it came to the point that they needed to sell. These same people can afford a lower payment at a fixed price, especially in regards to a rental. In fact, most of them may want to eventually purchase the property from you once they get their credit back in good standing.

Another opportunity that exists in a down market is an influx of government-subsidized tenants, which means government checks pay the rent. In 20+ years, I have never had a government check bounce. Many of the government programs are a pain to deal with. They are paperwork intensive and lots of the tenants have bad attitudes. However, there is a huge demand in this niche. One of the most well-known programs is "Section 8 housing," also called the "voucher program." There are also many other programs available; this is just the one I am most familiar with.

In my opinion, the downside to government programs is usually the yearly inspections. We have found that the inspectors tend to be very tough on the property when it is in a nice area, and very lenient when the property is located in a bad area. This frustrates us because it means the system is flawed. On the positive side, the checks are always on time from the government, although the tenant's portion is very seldom on time. This is okay since the government might be paying as much as 90 to 95 percent of the rent. In fact, in some situations they may pay 100 percent. The best part of the program is that there are more tenants than landlords in the program.

Foreclosures

The last part I want to cover on how to make money in a down market is using the government to fund your rentals by financing your rental properties. During down markets, the government may have many HUD and VA foreclosures. I am going to focus here on the VA foreclosures as a way to pick up great rental properties.

First of all, these properties tend to have equity. After the housing bubble burst in 2008, the VA had a program whereby investors could buy VA foreclosure properties with only 5% down and a 30-year, 4.x% fixed interest rate. As investors, this was a dream come true because when we go to the bank to get a loan, we are typically required to put down twenty percent or more. Therefore, five percent down for a VA foreclosure property was definitely an attractive alternative.

None of the foreclosed properties that we purchased through the VA needed much work. The repairs required were mostly cosmetic. These houses were usually cared for, and located in great neighborhoods. We found that these were usually foreclosed properties that had been empty six months to a year before they were placed on the MLS to be sold.

One other attractive element of purchasing a VA foreclosure is if you do so as the homeowner. If you buy the property and live in it yourself, it may be possible to get in with *zero* down payment! This is exactly how I got started in the '80s; I purchased a foreclosed property from the VA as a homeowner. I'd live in the property for a year, and then purchase another one from them to live in while putting the one I was currently in up for lease. This is how I started my rental business. In fact, back in the '80s, it was only $500 down and a 9% fixed rate loan.

There are other ways to make money in a down market. The purpose here is to give you some basics to get you motivated and thinking about how you can make money. Just remember that you're going to have a lot of folks telling you that you've lost your mind for investing in real estate when the market is bad. More than likely, these same naysayers will be telling you to buy real estate when the market is good and getting to the height of the peak just before the big dip. At that point, I want you to sell them all the inventory you have. Then, after the market finally does crash, odds are you'll be able to buy it back at a deeply discounted price.

I know it sounds counterintuitive, but you must understand we are investors: we do the opposite of what everyone else is doing, or telling us to do. We get in the real estate market when it's bad (low), and get out when it's great (high). It's almost like buying stocks except that the cycle does not occur daily; it occurs every ten to fifteen years. It is much easier to see the changes coming, which makes it easier for us to get paid by investing in real estate during down markets.

Many of those people who lost their homes to foreclosure during the collapse of the housing market are now re-entering the housing market as buyers. Of those, there's quite a few purchasing their home from the landlord they've been renting from for the last few years. Why? Interest rates during 2016, and now in the beginning of 2017 are at historically low levels, and it's a hot seller's market in many areas. The term "buy low, sell high" benefits both the buyers and sellers at this time.

Changing Market

What do you do when the market is rising and investors everywhere have become motivated buyers? It seems everyone has just started buying any and everything for very high prices. You go to the tax sales and the properties sell for not only more than the tax value, but many times more than the comps… and the buyers have not even been inside the properties.

Yet I see and know a lot of seasoned investors out there that are diversified in their investing strategies. We refuse to become Motivated Buyers. However, not everyone has that luxury. Most investors seem to have only one or two exit strategies and that's it. They have a limited number of tools in their financial tool belt that they're able and willing to utilize. I have been a real estate investor for over 30 years. What you need to keep in mind is you need many different exit strategies to be successful in real estate investing. You need to know how to wholesale real estate when the equity is there to do so. You need to be able to buy and hold properties to generate income on a monthly basis.

You also need to know the most popular exit strategy these days is to buy, fix and sell, but you need a lot of equity to do that. If you have the funds available, another good strategy right now is to invest in notes as there are good deals currently available. They may not be local to you but keep an eye out for them. Some notes may have a lot of equity in them, so if something goes wrong you actually may end up with that property and a lot of equity.

As a real estate investor you need to be able to adjust to the market conditions as they change. Invest in properties that have exit strategies that work for you now. You may also consider opening an IRA to wholesale, sell, or buy rentals and notes with. This way you are also building your wealth for the future.

Currently, my local market has gone nuts. If you're in a similar market, this can work to your advantage if you want to sell some inventory. I am selling a lot of my inventory, and if possible I try and sell via owner financing with large down payments to investors. There seems to be a lot of buy and hold investors in my market now from outside the state.

If you are a newbie to the investing arena it's going to be tough, however there are ways to get paid. You will first need to know all you can about real estate investing, so you may need to get some training. You are going to have to be able to move really fast when a deal pops up. **Realize you will have lots of competition in the market right now**. That is why I teach my students to stay away from MLS listings in this market and focus on areas such as probates that have not even been filed or petitioned for probate in the courts yet. There is less competition in Probates and you usually can get more time to work the deal which will help new investors be able to wholesale them. I started out as a wholesaler many years ago and still do it today. What I like about it is I did not need any money to get it done. Keep in mind if the market does bust then the wholesale game becomes the best exit strategy ever, again!

The main thing is position yourself so you can maneuver positively no matter where the market turns. If you keep your eyes on the market and not so much on the quick buck, you can become very successful at this real estate game!

Not so much on the quick buck, you can become very successful at this real estate game!

What Makes a Deal Good
In over 20 years of investing, mentoring and training, the most loaded question I receive is, "What makes a deal good?" Everyone has different criteria. For us, a deal is a property that has all the criteria we're looking for: a motivated seller, a distressed situation and poor property condition. Add it all up; put it in the right market situation, and bingo, we have a possible deal.

Motivated Seller
Motivated sellers are the key to a great deal. We need a seller who is willing to be open to any creative ways we come up with to solve their problem. If a seller is not motivated, it makes our job much harder. In fact, I generally don't pursue those properties any further because if the seller is not truly motivated, he may flip-flop on issues while in contract negotiations. I have always said that for them to be a motivated seller, they must have a problem they cannot solve by themselves. This does not mean taking advantage of someone who is in a desperate situation. Remember, we are problem solvers. This allows us the opportunity to help solve their problem. We get paid for this service, just like they would pay for any other service. Therefore, having a truly motivated seller is the first step in determining if a deal is good.

Poor Property Condition
The next factor we look for is a property in poor condition, or with problems that the owners cannot or will not fix themselves. This is where we have the opportunity to increase equity. Most owners do not have a clue what repairs their property really needs, or what it takes to bring the property up to compliance with current codes. Electrical, plumbing, and structural systems must meet these codes. This is where having a good home inspector on your team is invaluable. All of these repairs add up, and must be taken into consideration when negotiating an offer. In the seller's eyes, everything may work, so there's no problem. They don't understand that when the property sells on a new loan, it must pass certain conditions.

Here again, you must be the problem solver, and if you don't know what the property needs to pass all the needed inspections, it's likely the seller doesn't know either. Lenders have certain standards the property must meet before they will issue financing and funding on it. There are also many areas where the property must have a certificate of occupancy issued on it before utilities can be turned on or a tenant can move in. Usually, the property must meet current building codes before the city will issue such a permit.

Any time you get into a situation involving repairs, building codes, and major rehabbing, you have an opportunity to make a large profit. As an investor, you will learn to get these repairs done at a fraction of what it would cost a homeowner by having good contractors on your team, and thus receive better pricing. Understand that these lower contractor prices may be negotiated over time, as you develop relationships with the contractors and provide them ongoing business. The difference between the retail and discount prices of repairs actually becomes part of your profits. I love when property owners get bids or estimates on the repairs from companies that charge full retail prices to do the work. It helps our negotiations because they now have a bid which is significantly higher than what we, as investors, may be able to get the same work done for.

In my "Fast Track to Wholesaling" class, we talk a lot about getting information on repairs from the seller. We want to see any bids or estimates they already have. Even more importantly, we want their opinion as to what the repair costs will be, even if they have not obtained any estimates. I actually like it when they do not have any bids because many sellers think the necessary repairs we go through line by line are much more expensive than they really are. As investors, it is not our job to give them repair estimates or to even correct their ideas of what repairs cost – that is for a contractor to do. We just need to make sure they understand that there are repairs needed, and those repairs may possibly cost as much or more than they think.

The real point of going through these repairs with the seller is not to show them how much they may have to spend or how much they do not know about rehabbing. It is to test their motivation. If the seller gets irritated at going through all of the questions on our call script sheets, they are not motivated. If, however, they willingly give you all the information and details you seek, then – voilá! – you may have a motivated seller who now understands that the property may need more work than they are willing to deal with themselves.

Distressed Situation

Next, we look for a "distressed" situation; does the owner *have* to sell? I do not want to negotiate with someone who would just *like* to sell. I don't feel that the need, i.e. the motivation, is there. I want to work with a seller who *has* to sell, and has to sell yesterday! This is a situation that may present opportunity for us. At this point, you may be thinking that I am a somewhat callous businessman, but I'm not. I have just learned over the years that the most valuable thing in my life is my TIME! I do not want to waste it trying to get someone who is not motivated to sell me their property below value. Remember, as investors, we are problem solvers. We want to work with a seller who, due to the situation they find themselves in, needs us to buy their property now so that they can move on with their lives. It must be a win-win condition for both parties, or it's not a deal. They get relief from a bad state of affairs and we get paid.

Through the years, I have learned that sometimes we want to do a deal so badly that we actually become a motivated buyer. In the long run, this will cause you to end up frustrated and broke. We cannot help everyone. We can, however, help those who are in a situation that permits us to procure a property below its comparative market value, in a condition that most others would not attempt to tackle, and allow us to get paid at the same time as helping someone that others could not. My friends, this is much easier than trying to make an unmotivated seller motivated. Work with those who already are. In the long run, it will be the best use of the most valuable asset you have ever been given: TIME.

Making Money with No Money-

Purchasing Property

This is where I start to lose people and fear starts to set back in, so listen up: NO FEAR! I know some of you may be dead broke, have terrible credit, and cannot qualify for a loan to buy a property. Right now, you are telling yourself, "It sounds great, if I only had the money to actually buy a good deal when I see it." Let me set your mind at ease so that you can get rid of the negative thoughts and concentrate on finding deals. More than likely, at first you are not going to buy any properties yourself! Yes, you read that right: we are not going to have you starting out buying real estate, especially since you are probably broke. You see, we are actually Deal Finders. What we are going to start out doing is putting property **under contract** to buy, find a buyer that needs a deal, and then we sell them our contract for a fee. It's a strategy called wholesaling, which we will cover more in depth in Chapter 7. As you become more familiar with real estate investing and build up some funds to do it with, then you can move into the other exit strategies of Buy, Fix and Sell (Chapter 8) and Buy, Fix and Hold (Chapter 9).

What Do I Do First?

For now, let's talk about putting a contract on a piece of real estate: finding a deal and then entering into a contract to buy it.

Understand the Contract

At the time of this writing, anyone of legal age in the United States can contract to buy a piece of real estate without being a licensed real estate agent or broker. You can also sell a piece of real estate without being an agent or broker, but you must have a stake in the property to do so (i.e. you control the property via contract or deed). In fact, you don't even have to use a state board of realtors' contract; you can get a contract at your local office supply store if you so choose. I personally like to use the state board of realtors' contract because it's familiar to most people.

Although you can download a purchase contract from your state real estate board website (no, you don't have to be an agent to get it), you should get it from the title company you plan to do business with. Meet with the escrow officer who will be handling your transactions. Have them walk you through filling out a contract. This is a fairly simple procedure, but can be intimidating if you have no prior experience. It is also a great way to get to know your escrow officer and find out exactly he or she needs to make the closing process go smoothly.

You can usually find a good title company at your local real estate club. Be prepared to interview several companies though; let them know you will be doing assignments, double closings and wraps. Make sure they have experience processing these types of transactions. Many title companies are not used to doing these types of closings, so you want a company that works with investors and understands the different types of transactions you will be doing.

A word of warning when dealing with title companies, real estate agents, and brokers: many times you will find those that tell you, "You can't do that; it's illegal." What they're really saying is they don't know how to do the types of transactions you're using. Network with your local investors and real estate clubs. Ask the seasoned investors who they use, then use the same professionals. I have done this for over twenty years, and we still have people tell us all the time that we cannot do that. It's funny because our CPAs and attorneys, as well as the IRS are all familiar with it. They just all want to get paid for their involvement in it.

There are also real estate clubs that conduct weekend seminars on contracts and market conditions in your area. Go to them; learn and network. If they charge for the class, so what? It's like going to a two or three-day mini-college course at a fraction of what a college course would cost. Remember Hosea 4:6: "My people are destroyed from lack of knowledge." The biggest mistake I see beginning investors make is not getting the knowledge they need to be successful. They either don't get it at all, or try to save a few bucks by going to what I call "cheapy" training. My dad always said you get what you pay for. It's better to pay upfront for quality training so you get adequate information to start with than to end up paying a lot more down the road after you've made mistakes.

Become familiar with your local board of realtors' contract, or whichever contract you plan to use. Don't let filling out a contract scare you. Overcome the fear by asking for help. Let the escrow officer or other knowledgeable investors guide you in filling it out. Most of all, don't worry. Most contracts have one or more mistakes when they're filled out. The title company will help you make any needed corrections when you take it in to open escrow. They will go through it to make sure they understand it; the contract is the title company's set of instructions from the Buyer and Seller for the transfer of property.

Okay, let's move on. You now have no fear of contracts, and no fear of investing. Let's find some Motivated Sellers!

Motivated Sellers: the Key to Great Deals

The key to great deals is finding a motivated seller. These are sellers who want to solve a problem, and may need your help to do so. For instance, a property owner who is under pressure to bring their mortgage current may be a motivated seller.

Foreclosures

No matter what the economic market may be, there will always be some foreclosures. Bad things happen, even to good people. Death, divorce, medical bills, loss of job, tanking economic market conditions – there are many reasons that someone may enter into the foreclosure process.

During the last economic downturn in 2008-2012, there was an extreme uptick in home foreclosures. At the time, more than 30% of all loans were adjustable rate mortgages, more commonly known as ARMs. By 2009, there was an average of one of every ten mortgages either in default or behind on their mortgage payments. The "mortgage bubble" was caused in part by banks providing loans to those who really shouldn't have been able to qualify, and consumers were purchasing higher-priced properties than they could actually afford.

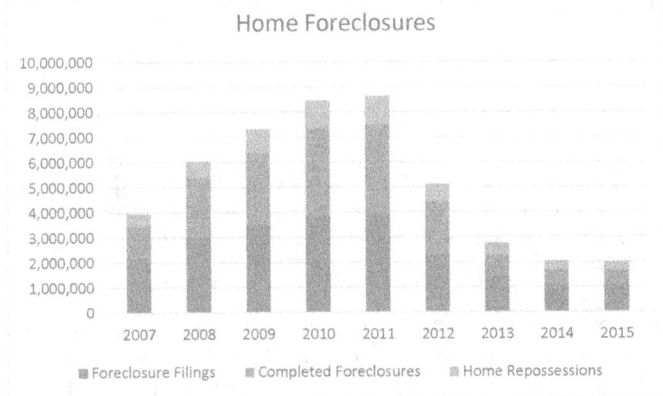

"Home Foreclosure Statistics – Statistic Brain."
2017 Statistic Brain Research Institute, publishing as Statistic Brain.
October 30, 2016
http://www.statisticbrain.com/home-foreclosure-statistics/

Keep in mind that many had ARM loans long before this bubble burst. The difference was that during that few years leading up to the collapse of the mortgage industry, standards had been decreased for qualifying – if an applicant could "fog a mirror" and "state their income" without proof, they could get some kind of loan. This was not all the banks' faults, though. Consumers did not pay proper attention to the loan documents they were signing. They either did not understand, or just chose to ignore the fact that the rates would adjust higher in x number of years.

As the adjustable rates went up, their mortgage payments went up several hundred dollars a month. Taxes went up almost every year too, based on (sometimes inflated) appraisal values. Homeowners could not make those new payments. This led to a collapse of the housing market. If these same people had purchased a smaller, cheaper, even older home for less money, they most likely would have been able to afford the increase in their monthly mortgage payments.

This is what I did when I bought my first two homes; I purchased way below value at wholesale prices, fixed them up, and moved into the first one for five years. I found another great deal, purchased that one, fixed it up, moved into it, and rented out the first one. I lived in the second one about ten years. When I sold it, I made a large profit on it, and because it was my home, I did not have to pay taxes on the profit. This allowed me to purchase the home I live in now. By only buying what I could comfortably afford at the time, fixing it up over time, then later selling it for a profit was I able to accomplish this. By the way, the home I am in now needed more work than the first two houses and five of the rentals I purchased combined. It was a real mess, but what a DEAL!

Keeping Up With the Joneses

Many Americans tend to live paycheck to paycheck and just too far above their means, so as rates adjusted, once manageable mortgage payments became impossible to keep up with. The issue we face in this country is the "We want it now!" syndrome. We are willing to leverage ourselves way above what I call "contentment." We want more than we really need or are able to afford. I have in the past called this "keeping up with the Joneses" which, simply put, means we want what others have no matter the price.

One thing I can tell you is that most people are never content. As soon as they get what they want, they decide they must have something else to be content. This is the reason I created my "Debt Free/Stewardship" training program. I designed it to help people get out of debt, live below their "contentment" levels, and use real estate as a tool to build a retirement portfolio for the future. I would suggest any of you who want to make a change in your life and build a future for your children's children take my Debt Free training. It is a free 9-hour, online course. You'll need to purchase the book that accompanies the course, but the videos are free. I know some will not want to pay for the book, but it will take approximately three times longer to complete the course if you do not have it. To put it in perspective, many people have no problem spending money on dinner out, but are not willing to spend the same amount on something that could not only help them get out of debt, but could put them on the path to becoming wealthy.

Senior Citizens

Another scenario that creates motivated sellers is probate. This is a tool that I use to find very motivated sellers. Most probates involve family members who have inherited a problem they need us to solve.

It's a little known fact that over 70% of the people in this country do not have a will. With or without a will, when you die your estate must go through probate. If you want to avoid your assets going through this process, then have an entity own them. You see, entities do not die; people do!

This has been such a great tool in my real estate investing career that one of my former students and I created an entire training program around acquiring real estate deals through probate. What we like most about this method is that there is very little competition. Probate is a guaranteed source of inventory because everyone will die someday. Therefore, take care of your family by preparing for their inheritance now! By the way, here's a clue about probate: the owner in probate is usually the one who passed away, so he no longer has a problem. However, his heirs may have one. For more detailed information on finding real estate deals in probate, check out my Probate training on my website www.JimmyReed.net. You might be surprised how good it can be!

Senior citizens and their families may also become motivated sellers when it becomes necessary for the aged person to enter into a nursing home. I know you may think this is crossing the line; however, in America, we tend to put our elderly family members in nursing homes when we cannot care for them ourselves. Many times, the people going into nursing homes have assets they have to get rid of so that government agencies, such as Medicaid, Medicare, Social Security and others will cover the nursing home expenses. Why, you ask? Many programs will not cover any costs as long as the person in the nursing home has assets that could generate money to pay those costs. It's sad but true that in this country, the government requires you to be dead broke before they're willing to give you any help. I have also learned that nursing homes work hand in hand with Social Services and Guardians.

Distressed Condition/Location

Another reason people become motivated sellers is that they have property in a distressed condition and/or location. Many homeowners would like to sell their property quickly at a discount; however, the condition of the property is so bad that no retail homebuyers will even make an offer on it. Even if the potential homebuyer is willing to make some repairs, most need a bank loan, and banks do not tend to make loans on properties in bad condition. Voila, Super Motivation! You have a seller who cannot sell their property unless someone is willing to buy it for all cash! This is what we are looking for; a property we can buy far enough below retail value, factoring in repairs, and make a cash offer to the sellers that they will not usually be able to refuse. Again, we did not create the situation, but we might be able to solve it. That is the key to a motivated seller, and thus, a great deal.

Property conditions are not always as terrible as "oh, we've got to bulldoze it," or "it's been condemned by the city." In most cases, the repairs needed are electrical, plumbing or foundation issues. The property can be fixed up; it's just that the owners do not have the ability or funds to make the repairs themselves so they must sell the property in "as is" condition! This is where you can make really good money in real estate.

Most people do not have a clue as to what the costs of repairs are or where to get the right bids. The property owners do not usually work with wholesale contractors; vendors who work with investors on a regular basis and at a much lower price. These contractors do this because they know the investors can give them lots of work. Even if we are not buying the property with the intent to repair it ourselves, we know that the cash buyers we sell the property to will use the same contractors to do the work. By the way, you need to add contractors to your database as you will more than likely need their services at some point. One place to find them is at your local real estate club; the best place for networking.

Location is a factor the seller cannot change, yet may be the main reason they want to sell. The property may be in an area with no demand by homeowners. It may be in an area that has demand, but the potential homeowners cannot qualify for a loan. Some areas have declined in demand due to changing trends, such as population, job availability or crime. In these instances, there is not a demand for retail homebuyers.

There is, however, a demand from buyers who would like to be homeowners but do not have the necessary credit to qualify. If structured correctly, this can be a great deal for the investor willing to buy this property from you and then resell it to the person who either has bad or no credit. Investors will sell to these homebuyers because, in many areas, these end buyers have a substantial amount of cash for a down payment, but no credit to get a bank or mortgage loan. This owner finance technique is very popular in lower income and working class areas. The best part is that most people would not even consider selling the property this way themselves, even if they could get more for the property. This is great for investors because we'll do these kinds of deals all day long.

The possibilities are growing. Keep in mind, in all of the scenarios above we did not create the problems, we are just trying to solve them. There have been, and will always be, motivated sellers. Our goal is to find those people that need help, have deals, and are willing to sell them to us at a significant discount for cash. There are many other techniques for finding motivated sellers. I teach about twenty of them in my "Fast Track to Wholesaling" training class.

Power Team
By the way, you will want knowledgeable professionals to be part of what I call your "Power Team." These are the people who will guide you on how to set up entities, how to do your taxes, and will also keep you up to date on any changes in the law that may affect you. A great team is necessary to become a successful real estate investor, and may take some time to put together. After the escrow officer, you should obtain the services of a good CPA who is used to dealing with real estate-related business. They can guide you regarding who else and what else you may need to succeed in this business.

Title Company
Find the title company you plan on working with. It should be one that has experience doing assignments, double closings and wraps; works with investors; and knows what you are trying to accomplish.

Realtor
Many realtors do not like working with investors because we make such low offers. You want an agent on your power team who understands the industry from an investor viewpoint, and will present all of your offers to sellers no matter how low they may be. A good agent will work not only with homebuyers, but will also love working with investors. They understand that investors are repeat buyers; we buy everyday whereas homebuyers only buy once every so many years. A great broker/agent knows that volume is better for sales over the long haul. If you currently have an agent that is not willing to work with you as an investor, then head to your local real estate club. I am sure you will find some who will be more than happy to do so.

There are many others you will need such as CPA, Real Estate Attorney, for sure a good Real Estate Club, but for now let's focus on getting the main team and getting you paid!

What Do You Do When You Get a Deal?

Remember when I talked earlier about controlling real estate? This is what happens when we put a piece of property under contract to buy; we are controlling it. We have tied the property up with a purchase contract that has some specific terms which have been agreed upon by both the Seller and the Buyer. Typically, we have negotiated a price, either for cash or with terms. We have agreed to take the property in its present condition so as to get a better price. We have also agreed to take the problem off of the Seller's hands within 30-45 days of acceptance of the contract by both parties.

Purchasing a Property: Contracts – Initial Offer to Closing

Let's start at the point where we have already talked to a motivated seller who most likely found us through our marketing campaign on "We Buy Houses CASH." We have negotiated a price and the seller has agreed to sell us the property. Now, we set up a time to meet with them and sign a Purchase Contract Agreement. Again, I suggest you use the local board of realtors' contract.

Escape Clause

Most importantly, we made sure there is a provision in the contract that allows us to walk away completely if we find something that hinders us from wanting to close. I call this particular clause my "Subject-To Clause." This is not the same as buying a property "subject to" existing notes, such as is done in short sales. This "Subject-To" is in regards to the condition, title, financing and other miscellaneous issues with the property. Many also know it as an "Escape Clause." It's a clause that allows you to back out of a contract for any reason stated. This is where being very familiar with your local board of realtor's contract will be invaluable – some already have these provisions in them, especially during an option period, and some will need a provision added. (Be sure to contact the real estate attorney on your power team for the exact legal wording that is appropriate for the market you are working in.)

Of course, the reason we are most concerned with here as a wholesaler is, "Can I find someone with cash who will pay me more than I have it under contract for?"

If I am purchasing the property to fix and sell, or fix and hold, I am most concerned with "What repairs need to be made, and how much will they cost, so that I can purchase at a price that will allow me to make a profit when sold or cash flow when rented?"

Contract to Title Company

Once the seller signs the contract, the first thing to do is to fax or email it to the escrow officer at the title company that is handling all of your assignments and double closings. There are three main reasons for this. First, we want to make sure there are no issues on the title that would prevent us from selling once we have a buyer ready to close. The second reason is that you don't want to upset the cash investor by having them come to the closing only to find out it was a wasted trip because the title is not clear. The third reason is that if there is a problem with the title, you need to find out as soon as possible so that it can be straightened out before closing. Many students forget this part of their training and end up losing their deal at the last minute whereas, if they had given the title company sufficient time to work, the title could have been cleared and the deal completed.

Choosing Your Exit Strategies

You *must* have clear exit strategies defined for a property *before* you ever buy it.

Wholesale

Wholesaling is the bread and butter of real estate investing 101! It is the strategy you use to move a property quickly without having to use any money of your own to do so. Wholesaling is the easiest place for a novice investor to begin learning.

Our intent starting out is not to close on the property ourselves. There is a difference in placing a contract on a property, and closing on a property. Closing requires CASH! The rule is we make our money when we buy, or when we control a property under contract. Once we have some equity and a motivated seller, then we are a step away from having a deal. Of course, this is where new investors get excited and scared all at the same time. You see, until we actually sell the contract, we only have control of the deal. Our goal is to get paid! We must have wholesale buyers, i.e., investors, who can close quickly and pay all cash. This is a concern for new investors who do not have a database full of buyers. The good news is that where there is a deal, there soon will be cash. The key is to let everyone know you have a deal for sale as soon as you get it.

Negotiate price with investor

For now, let's keep it simple and assume we have a signed contract with necessary escape clauses added in. Our escape clause/option period will let us exit for whatever reason within a prescribed period of time. Let's also assume that we have said we would close in 30-40 days, and that our option period, that allowed us to back out for whatever reason, is between 10-14 days (this will be dependent on your market, your seller's motivation, and what you can negotiate.)

Test Marketing

Once the contract is signed, we need to let the seller know we might put a sign up in the front yard to do some "test marketing." Remember, if they are truly motivated and need to get rid of their problem, this will not be an issue. We also want access to the property so inspections and bids can be prepared. We will not be getting these done ourselves; it will be the investor we are selling to getting them completed, and at his own cost. The escape clauses are for us to use to back out, but the bids and inspections are things our end user (our investor) really needs to be able to do on the property.

Next we start marketing the property so as to find an investor who is able to pay all cash for it. Once we have someone who is interested, we set up a time to meet them at the property, allow them to look around, and see if they are ready to proceed by making an offer. Our asking price, as used in our marketing, should be a few thousand dollars more than what we have it under contract with the seller for. However, you never ask so much that it is not a deal for our end user: the investor. If you do, the likelihood of someone calling your office to make an offer on it is slim. It's better to make a small profit than none at all. Our goal is to get paid, provide our investor a great deal, then move on and find another one that our investor will buy from us next month.

Assignment or double close
We now have the property under contract, we have a very favorable asking price so as to attract the attention of an investor, and now we are meeting them to see if they want to proceed forward with an offer. Once they make an offer, it's simple to decide which type of closing is the best one to use. To keep it simple for the purposes of this book, use the following guidelines starting out. If your fee is $3,000 or less, use an *assignment*. If your fee is over $3,000, then use a *double close*. In my two-day wholesale training, we role play this quite a bit as we delve into the reasoning behind the differences, but for now, just stick with the rule until you have more experience. Keep in mind that as you become a better investor, this rule will change. This is why my training is called "Fast Track to Wholesaling."

If you're going to assign the property to your investor, you will use an Assignment Contract. If you opt for a double close, then you will need another Purchase Contract. This is just like the one you have with the original seller, except that now you are listed as the seller and your investor is listed as the buyer. At this point, we could spend hours here going over the details of each type of closing, but it would be more confusing than helpful to you. Instead, I highly recommend that you either go to your local real estate investment club and network with some seasoned investors who can help you in this area, or go to a live seminar. This way you can see firsthand how it's done, plus you'll have the opportunity to ask questions.

The reason I do live trainings is because people can watch us go through this process in our role-playing, and we can draw it out in a flowchart format so it's easy to understand. Then we do Q&A in it, for hours if necessary, so that by the time we are done, the entire class really understands it. In fact, I don't leave the class until they do. A really good live training course may have a small initial cost up front to attend, but it can save you lots of money and time in the long run!

Second contract to title
Once our investor has made an offer and we have accepted it, we use one of the techniques above to put it in writing. We then email or hand-deliver the signed contract over to our title company so they can prepare the necessary paperwork for closing. This is where we need to have a great title company on our team. We must have an escrow officer who understands, and has done plenty of assignments and double closings. Until we have closed and funded, we have

not gotten paid, and we do not want something going wrong just because we are not working with the right title company.

At closing, if we have done an assignment, we will have very little paperwork to complete. However, if we do a double closing, there will be much more paperwork involved. It will be just as if we were purchasing the property ourselves, which we actually are even though it's for a short period of time. Don't stress over it though; your escrow agent will walk you through it. After all, this is when you get paid!

If for any reason your investor decides not to close, or you get no offers within the first two weeks, simply back out of the contract and move on to the next deal. This is why you have an escape clause in your contract. You must realize that not every deal is going to work. However, if you negotiate a good deal upfront so that it is a win for the seller, you, and your investor, and you conduct business as a person of integrity by staying within the time-sensitive parameters you negotiate, you shouldn't have to back out very often. This is real life investing!!!

Buy, Fix and Sell

This technique is for the more advanced investors. You need rehab experience and cash, or access to cash. You can also get very creative with this strategy by implementing owner financing, first and second liens, or utilizing money partners or hard money lenders.

Although it comes with more risk, rehabbing a property and then selling it on the retail market has the potential for the largest amount of profit. This is why many investors like the buy, fix and sell strategy. It's a great way to make big bucks if you learn how to do it the right way. Starting out, you may still want to wholesale some properties over to those investors that like to retail, go ahead and get paid, then watch and learn. Drop by the property to see how long it takes their crew to rehab. Look at the work they're actually doing. If you like the quality of what you see, introduce yourself to the contractors and get their contact information for future rehab jobs. This makes networking fun – you're making contacts you can use for future projects, and you know they work with investors. Heck, you just got them through the investor you sold the property to!

Find out from the investor what price they are asking for the property on the retail market, and how they are selling it. Is it on a new loan, or are they offering owner financing? There's a lot to learn about rehabbing, so you might as well get paid while you do it. Sometimes, I find such great deals that my wholesale fee is as much as the investor will make once he's sold the property. That's the fun part – making big bucks without any hard labor. I love wholesaling real estate; it truly is the bread and butter of investing.

What You Need to Know

Be aware that when you start into the rehab and retail end of real estate, you are definitely going to be doing some work. To be successful using this strategy, you must have a great support team that includes licensed electricians, plumbers and heating/air conditioning technicians. You will also need professionals who can frame, put up sheetrock, paint, and do great detail work. When you remodel a house, remember who your customer will be. More than likely it will be a homeowner, and they are very picky about what they buy. After all, this type of customer buys on emotion, so they must fall in love with the house in order to want to live there.

You will have to learn about building codes and permits, even if you obtain the services of a general contractor. A great investor will always learn about rehabbing from all perspectives – he'll know what wax rings and ground fault interrupt circuits are. Having this knowledge will enable you, the entrepreneur, to negotiate with your vendors for lower prices. You see, the more money you can save through negotiating lower costs while rehabbing a house, the more you can make when you finish the project and sell it to the new homeowner.

Learn by Doing

When I started out, I did not know very much about remodeling a house. Over the years, I learned by doing it myself, sometimes doing it wrong, and spending way more than it would have cost if I had just hired a professional to do the job in the first place. However, I was on a tight budget starting out and did not have a lot of money to hire those professionals then. By taking a few arrows in the assets, I learned very quickly what to do and not do. I also learned it was not fun doing all of the hard manual labor myself. A friend once told me that the most powerful tool I had in real estate was my pen – used to write checks to pay those who could do the job better than me. I found out I could make more money by finding deals than by crawling under houses. I will say this though; experience is the best teacher. I learned a lot from all of those jobs I did myself. I learned how to negotiate with vendors from the standpoint of, "I've done that job and know what it takes and how much it costs to get it done." That knowledge and experience has been invaluable as I have built my company. It is still how I assess needed repairs and their costs when I am evaluating a property for purchase.

Over the years, I have told my students that the best way to learn about rehabbing and building a house is to go volunteer for a week with Habitat for Humanity. In the past, I have taken some of my bird dogs with me and my church group to volunteer for Habitat. We would learn more there in one day than you could learn at a month of attending rehab training classes or going to work for a builder. The week we built our first Habitat home, I learned all you need to know in remodeling and building. The work went up so fast that the city code enforcement and building permit officers came out daily to conduct inspections and show us if we had done anything wrong, or what codes we needed to know or had been changed. That experience was so valuable to us, and yet we were also able to help people who were in need of new homes. By the way, the homeowner also had to help build the house. I like that; it makes people be responsible and accountable for trying to make something of themselves. I love to be able to help people, especially those less fortunate, but I also want to see effort from them on their own behalf. That is what God wants to see from us too; that we at least attempt to do our very best and honor Him in all we do.

Habitat for Humanity is also a valuable resource for turning around blighted neighborhoods. These tend to be located in low income areas, usually near the downtown areas in most cities. This also presents an opportunity as an investor to pick up properties near these Habitat homes. We can rehab a house next door to a brand new construction property. This helps our comps, and provides the opportunity to sell to homeowners who wants nice houses around them, but can only afford to buy in a lower-income area. This piggy-backing technique in the lower-income areas is great even when all you want to do is wholesale the properties to other investors. Keep in mind that wholesaling is really the best way to start out in real estate, especially when you're dead broke.

Selling a Rehab

When calculating the costs analysis for a rehab project, you may want to consider adding in a fee for a realtor to resell the property to a homeowner for you. When I want to sell a home, I typically do it myself as a FSBO property, but I have many years' experience doing it. Starting out, I wish I would have used a realtor. They could have listed the properties in the MLS system, and thus reached a larger group of interested buyers. I know you have to pay a realtor commission, but if they can sell the property faster than you can, you will actually end up making more money. This is because you won't have as high carrying costs; i.e. financing or hard money fees, lawn care, insurance, utilities, property taxes, etc. Remember, time is your most valuable asset, and they can save you a lot of time by weeding out those who are "just looking" or can't qualify for whatever financing is available. Instead, you might even consider offering them a $500-$1,000 action bonus if they can get the property sold and closed within a certain timeframe. Think about it; if you offer a bonus to a realtor, whose house do you think might happen to end up at the top of the showing list?

The last major piece of selling retail is financing. In a hot market, it can be challenging, and in a down market, it can be really tough. It may even kill a deal because financing can fall through for a myriad of reasons at any time, right up to closing. Don't worry; a true investor has multiple exit strategies up his sleeve. If a loan falls through, you need to be prepared in advance. I call this scenario "What If?" What if financing falls through at the closing table? Did you run your initial numbers with some other exit strategies? By the way, you need this "what if" strategy when you buy, too.

My favorite exit strategy, especially for buy, fix and sell, is owner financing. I love this strategy because I actually become the bank, and the "Bank of Jimmy" processes loan applications in an hour, not months, and "Bank of Jimmy" can get instant loan approval the moment the buyer gives us a down payment. We close in a day, not four to eight weeks like the typical lending institutions. Once our homebuyer can show us they have ten to fifteen percent to put down, we are good to go.

Now you may be saying, "hold on 'Bank of Jimmy.' I do not have the ability to buy a property, fix it up and then only get a little bit of money down when I sell it." No problem; you just need to be good at running your numbers up front before you actually purchase the property. Let's look at this example:

Sample Deal

Purchase Price	$60,000
Rehab Cost	$15,000
Loan Cost	$ 9,000 this is money borrowed from a hard money lender at 12%

Total   **$84,000 to do the deal**

Let's say the property is worth $110,000 ARV (after repaired value) based on comparable sales as shown on the MLS. We now sell it with owner financing, and can actually get more than normal comps show. Why? We are selling with favorable terms. We find homeowners who want a house, have cash for a down payment, but have terrible credit. These buyers do exist in your markets. Many tend to be new to this country so they do not have credit, but they came here with cash. They are willing to pay more for a piece of the "American Dream" --home ownership. Let's say we sell them the house above for $120,000 with 10% down payment to us. Now we have $12,000 for the down payment, but it cost us $84,000 to do the deal, plus we have to pay that hard money lender within six months to a year. What do we do? We collect some payments for about three to six months and then we go to our network and find a note buyer.

Note buyers are investors who buy notes at a discount for all cash. You see, this is what your typical bank does as well. When you get a loan, they sell off your mortgage, usually within the first year, and at a discount. You still owe the same amount, but the new note holder collects your payment each month and has less invested in the property than what you owe. These note buyers like to have higher interest rates on the notes they buy than those rates charged to homeowners by conventional lenders. If the bank charges 4% on a new loan, we will charge about 8-9% owner financed. For someone who cannot qualify for a regular bank loan, this is a great deal.

Now we find a note buyer and sell our note to them at approximately 20% below value. Many factors are used to determine this discount. As each note buyer has their own guidelines of how they buy, so we will want several different offers. For this example, we will use the 20% discount. This equates to $120,000 sell price minus a down payment of $12,000, leaving a balance of $108,000. This $108,000 minus 20% discount to the note buyer is $86,400 cash they will give us for the note. We owed $84,000 back to the hard money lender for covering the purchase, rehab, and their fees to loan us the money. Therefore, we now have $2,400 left over after the discount. Then again, most likely this amount has been applied to closing costs, so we are basically even. Remember the $12,000 down payment we received when we sold the property to the homeowner? Oh yeah, that's ours. We just got paid $12,000 to do a deal with no money out of our own pocket. Not bad, not bad at all.

But wait; there is more. You need a good CPA on your team because when we sold that note at a discount, we actually lost $21,600. This means that we most likely have a write-off to factor in now on this deal. You heard me; a write-off. The value of the note was $108,000, but we let it go for $86,400, so we have a loss. I told you; you can make money in any market, and I bet you didn't know that Uncle Sam had a bonus waiting for you too!

This is just one possible way to make a deal work and get paid when others say it just will not work. You have to be creative in real estate investing. In my two and three day trainings, we always go over different exit strategies so our students have options. The more options you have, the more likely you can make a deal work and get paid. Keep in mind; I could come up with many more scenarios on this sample deal. We could do a first lien with a second lien, or some sort of wrap. We could keep one note and sell the other note. You can even sell just part of a note. The key is to have the knowledge at your fingertips to choose what works best for you.

I cannot encourage you enough to get some live training if you are struggling at trying to do some deals. Just make sure you take only the training you need. Otherwise, you're going to be going through so many different options that you will end up with what we call "analysis paralysis." If you wait too long to make the initial offer on the property you want because you're sorting through a plethora of options, the deal will be long gone by the time you finally make a decision.

Buy, Fix and Hold

The buy fix and hold strategy is the one that allows you to create long-term wealth. Over time, you can make a lot of money and have your tenants pay for your property. Not only is this strategy the most time-consuming, it is also the biggest fear many investors have to conquer. First, you must first overcome the fear. Many investors are scared to become wealthy because they can only see the negative side of this type of investment. They are focusing on the fact that they are buying a property with a loan on it, and worrying about turning around and renting it to someone for enough money to cover the loans, maintenance, taxes, and insurance, and still be generating a profit.

Again, the fear is based on that ole "What if?" What if it goes vacant? What if I cannot get it rented to cover the mortgage on time? These are legitimate concerns. Here is the "What if" I want to you answer first though. What if you do nothing at all to invest in your future? You see, entrepreneurs may feel the fear, but they will analyze the different scenarios and then take action. They are willing to take a calculated risk to improve their future. If you allow yourself to be paralyzed by fear and do not take action when opportunity presents itself, then you will never get ahead.

Does this mean you look at the world through rose-colored glasses and think you'll never have a problem? No. You carefully analyze the deal, assume the worst, know that there will be problems at some point, but over time, decide if the risk will make you wealthy. You see, we don't live in a perfect world. Eventually, you're going to have to pay for some repairs on a rental property. At some point in time, you're going to have vacancies, and will most likely have to make some of the mortgage payments on the investment.

As an investor, you must look at the big picture. Over time, factoring in the cash out of pocket and the rents coming in, plus all of the associated tax write-offs, is the investment going to make you money? Then we go one step further. Over time, will the property finally become free and clear? If you never refinance it or leverage it, then yes, you will eventually own it free and clear. Then you will have 100% equity available in a property that might be worth $100,000. Get ten of those and before you know it, your net worth is $1,000,000.

At that point, I know you may have had to invest more money into your property, but much of that may be tax deductible. You may have had some losses that ended up being beneficial to you from owning the property. Over time though, you should have had more positive cash flow than you did a negative loss. The ultimate goal is to eventually have ten nice homes that you own, free and clear, bringing in a larger net cash flow once you have finally paid off the loans. By the way, you could also tap the equity, getting access to immediate cash, by refinancing the loan. As we discussed earlier in the book, that cash may be tax-free. You might be able to let your IRA own the property as an investment. Then depending on the type of IRA you have, the profits you make over time could be either tax-deferrable or tax-free.

The basic concept of this strategy is that you are buying an asset that appreciates over time, and meanwhile someone else is paying off the note on it. When you have tenants, they are making the payment to you, hopefully for more than what your costs are. You do have to do some work; you have to buy the property, get it repaired and then manage it. If you want to let someone else handle the day-to-day management, that is fine, but you still need to manage the manager. No one will ever have a more vested interest in your properties than you do.

If you do manage your properties on your own, you have a new job. Let me tell you one thing you should never forget: managing tenants is like babysitting. You must know that end of the business; what laws you must obey, what rules you have to follow to do evictions, and what the requirements are to get a tenant out if they do not pay. You can learn all of this from attending local clubs or trainings on property management. I strongly suggest you at least take a course or read some books on it. However you choose to do it, you must obtain some knowledge in this aspect so you will not get yourself into any kind of trouble.

It is not my intent to scare you away from property management; but you need to be prepared if you decide to do it yourself. Should you decide to go and outsource the management, then find a good, reputable company that can do everything needed to make your property profitable. After all, this is your investment future and you want it to have the highest productivity possible in order to get the best return on your money.

One aspect of holding rental property that I really like is that there will always be a demand for it. You see, people will always need a place to call home. According to the 2010 U.S. Census, there are approximately 308.7 million people in the United States, of which 300.8 million live in 116.7 million households. The Bureau estimates that as of 2015, 42.2 million of these households, or over 36%, are renters! (Source: U.S. Census Bureau, 2011-2015 American Community Survey 5-Year Estimates) Out of this pool of renters, most would prefer living in a single family house over a multifamily dwelling. The great part about it is that those who can afford to rent a house can lease your property, and perhaps eventually buy it from you as well. Those who cannot afford to rent a house tend to live in multifamily complexes because of the price points. Therefore, if you want to hold some duplexes or apartments someday, then do it. No matter what type of rental property you have, there will be some kind of demand for it. That's what makes real estate such an attractive investment; it fills a demand that is also a human necessity.

Another aspect of holding rentals is that over time, you have the ability to sell them for a profit, and then utilize a 1031 tax exchange to buy one large property such as an apartment complex. The 1031 may keep you from having to pay taxes on your profit, and gets you into a larger density property, such as an apartment building, that may have a stronger and larger cash flow. (Be sure to consult with your CPA and real estate attorney on the proper exchange guidelines and procedures.) This can become one of the most strategic moves you could ever make in becoming a millionaire.

The right property in the right location, up and running with good management, strong cash flow, and good cash-on-cash return could have you set up to sell the apartments to an investor when you are ready to retire. However, you should sell it owner financed, take a 20–30% down payment on the sales price, and then hold the note with all that cash flow coming in for years to come. That's right; cash flow with no management is your reward for those years of working hard and keeping those rent houses full, selling them all off and utilizing the 1031 tax exchange to purchase a large multifamily building which you manage for a few years until the market appreciation starts to hit all time new highs, then, BAM! Sell it to another investor with terms so you now have no responsibilities and yet you reap the rewards of cash flow. By the way if they ever default, you take it back and sell it again: double BAM, BAM!

Folks, that's how millionaires are made in this country. Think about it. It all started with getting over that fear of "What If!" What if we fail, what if we get foreclosed on because we cannot make the payments? As an investor, these are all legitimate concerns but keep this in mind; if you did go into foreclosure and lose the property, what would really happen to you? Guess what? You just have a foreclosure on your now bad credit. About all that could really happen is they take the property away from you and leave you with bad credit and a foreclosure on your record.

How many millionaires out there do you think may have had a foreclosure or a bankruptcy before? I bet plenty, and the only thing they did was go out and try it again. You see, in real estate you do not need credit to buy property that is owner-financed. In fact, when the right deal comes along and it could make a lot of money, then bring in a money partner. I have worked with and seen many investors who do very well in this country with bad credit, no money, and a foreclosure or two on their records.

Don't misunderstand me; I do not endorse an "I don't care what happens" attitude, or one of "who cares if I go into default on everything? I'll just walk away." On the contrary, I just want to make sure you understand it sometimes happens, and you just move on and do your best. Look at Job in the Bible. At one time in his life, he lost everything. However, he kept on going and still declared that God was great. He did everything in faith and trusted God in the good times and bad. Later in his life, he was blessed twice as much as before he had lost everything. I just want you to try, and have some faith while trying.

In my Debt Free/Stewardship training we talk about how God loves for His people to take steps of faith. Even if we fail, we trust that He will lead us and guide us to do what He has planned for us. If you never try, you will never know what God may be ready to bless you with. Remember this: many great people in the Bible failed. They just had faith that could move mountains, so kept on failing forward and were therefore blessed.

To wrap this up, buy, fix, and hold can make you wealthy, if first you create cash by wholesaling or utilizing buy, fix and sell. With the cash you generate, you can buy some rentals. Over time they will most likely go up in value, and so should the associated cash flow. Then you can make a choice of "do I sell, pay my taxes, and retire?" or "do I sell, carry a note, and create income for another 20-30 years with no responsibilities?" Better yet, wouldn't you like to have to make that decision some day? If so, then it's time to get started now.

By the way, if you're wondering how strong rents are over a period of time, check out the graph below. You really do not see much of an up and down roller coaster effect when it comes to rentals. Tape it up on your wall to help give you a little more courage to go get that first one.

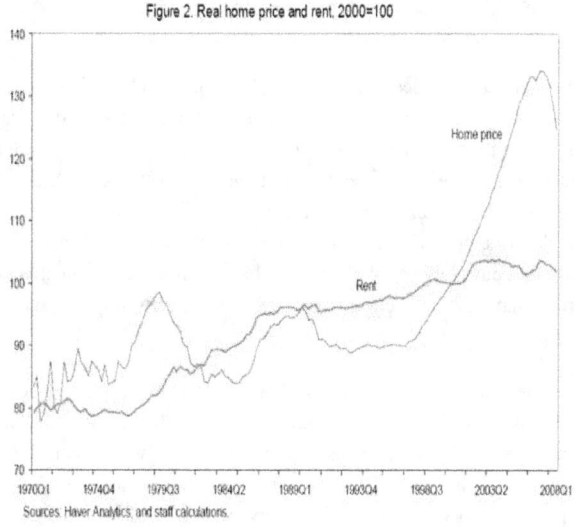

Figure 2. Real home price and rent, 2000=100
Sources: Haver Analytics, and staff calculations.

As you can see, rents generally go up over a period of time. There will always be a demand for rentals because so many people cannot afford nor even imagine ever owning a home. I want you to remember this when you sell to someone who thought they would never be able to buy a home until you showed them that with bank of _____ (Insert your name), their credit is as good as their down payment!

Marketing to Investors
Run an ad in the local newspaper, include the Social media versions, and other media sites, and make sure to include any online advertisements extras the paper has available.

Contact Your Database
Once the signed contract is turned into the title company, it's time to start a full-blow marketing campaign to let investors know you have a deal for sale. E-mail your entire database; let them know you have a phenomenal deal and the first person with cash gets it. Next, call all of the investors that use the "We Buy Houses" advertising in the papers and on bandit signs. Let them know you have a great deal so it won't last long. You can find these people by calling all of the corresponding ads in the local newspapers and weekly sale papers, such as Greensheet or Thrifty Nickel, as well as these publications' corresponding online ads. You can also find them by watching for billboards and bandit signs scattered around low and working class neighborhoods. As a side note, be sure you are considering your own marketing strategies for buying properties. You should run your own ads saying you buy houses, and put up signs and flyers with the same type of "We Buy Houses" marketing. This not only allows investors to contact you for deals they want to sell, but allows you to be able to sell to them as well.

Network
Be sure to put out flyers at your local real estate club. This lets all the investors there know you have a deal. It also lets them know you are an active investor, not just watching from the sidelines. Again, this is the best place to network and build a power team. Many clubs have a lot of money lenders and title escrow agents that attend the meetings. Ask them for referrals to investors they work with. You can even offer them a referral fee is their lead results in you being able to close a deal. It is, and will always be, about networking. When you look at the most successful investors in your area, you will see they have developed large networks. That is why it is vitally important that we extend our own networks in as many ways as possible.

Internet Marketing
Use "for sale" websites such as Craigslist, Facebook, YouTube, and any other service you can find that gets the word out to investors you have a fantastic deal available. The fastest way to network is the internet, and you can just about reach the whole world via social media networking. Forums such as Linked In, Facebook, Twitter, Instagram, YouTube and many others can be utilized to build your network in cyberspace.

McDonald's of Real Estate
Many new, and sometimes even seasoned, investors make the mistake of getting so overwhelmed with calls that they stop marketing for a time to catch up. This is a big no-no; you *never* stop marketing. Your goal is to become the McDonald's of real estate. You want to be the first person people think of when they think of real estate investing just as they think of

McDonald's when they think of hamburgers. You see, McDonald's is always marketing, no matter the economic reality of the moment. McDonald's lets everyone know if that if you want a burger, they've got one for you. If you were to ask anyone in the world, "Who is McDonald's?" you would get a correct answer eight out of ten times. The reason is because they never stop marketing. They know that you may not come to them every time you want a burger, but they also know if they market enough, you will walk through their doors at some point.

It is the same with real estate marketing. We have to continually market no matter what the current economic situation is. We must have not only an endless list of buyers, but at the same time need a steady supply of wholesale investors and motivated sellers. Therefore, our marketing must be two-fold. We need successfully targeted marketing campaigns for both buyers and sellers. Once you are the investor known for buying and selling real estate, then you will also be the one doing all the deals and making all the money.

Your Website

As soon as you can, you'll want to have your own website. Once you develop the right marketing, you can actually train your investors to go here on a daily basis to find information on deals you currently have available. By putting information on your deals on the website, you are answering the same questions for all of your investors at the same time. This allows you to spend your one-on-one time with investors actually putting deals together. Get them trained that deals and opportunity only lasts for five minutes, so they better be on your website daily looking to see what you have available because the deals won't last long!

You can actually create opt-in programs to collect your investors' information whenever they hit your websites. This will allow you to then be able to market deals by sending a broadcast e-mail to all of the investors at once, letting them know what you have and the first one that contacts you that can close the deal gets it. I love this method or networking and marketing. We do not have to spend as much time selling, so we have more time to find more deals. This, in turn, helps us streamline our business while increasing our cash flow, allowing us to spend more time focused on other areas. We can also conduct business no matter where we are, as long as we have access to our computers and an internet connection.

In our company, we feel that videos are becoming the main internet source for giving out information. Nowadays, you can buy a cheap pocket camcorder to shoots videos of your property deals, along with any repairs they need. You can then upload the videos to your website, e-mail them to your investors, or both. Our company is using this method of getting word out to investors fast via the following websites:

- www.JimmyReed.net This is our main web page with all our real estate deals, trainings, and a list of special events. We also offer links to some of our network vendors that we use and encourage our investors to use.

- http://www.youtube.com/user/jimmyvreed This is where we use videos to let investors know about real estate tips, trainings we are doing, and to just let them get to know us a little better.

- http://www.linkedin.com/in/jimmyreed A lot of investors use the networking tool as their main data contact; we use it as our internet network contact. We use this tool mainly because so many other investors like it. I actually prefer the next one for fast up-to-the-minute networking.

- http://twitter.com/jimmyreeddotnet This one can wear you out, but it can also keep you updated on the latest things happening within your network the moment it happens. Use the cell phone and texting formats as the primary ways to keep in touch. I like to send what is known as a "tweet" when I have a deal THE SECOND I SIGN THE CONTRACT! Now, that is fast. My investors have a shot to get it before I have ever faxed it to the title company or even had a chance to put it on my website.

- http://www.google.com/profiles/JimmyVReed Google is the most popular search engine on the internet. We have a Google account that is set up mainly to drive people to our website or one of the sites above to get them into our network.

- http://www.facebook.com/jimmyreeddotnet Facebook has become one of the fastest and most popular networking sites. Although it is not really how I like to keep in touch with my friends, a lot of people like this format so we use it.

At this point, you might be thinking, "How in the heck am I ever going to keep up with all of these sites, and still get any work done?" We have even more sites than these, and I can tell you it became very difficult until we found about http://www.ping.fm. This tool allows me to send the same message to most of my sites simultaneously. This way, I only have to update a few sites instead of fifteen or more.

We have other internet sites, but again, this is just a sample to show you how we are focusing our marketing campaign. We also offer FREE gifts for investors and students when they join our network via our main webpage. Once they sign up, we send them free real estate articles as well as a link to get the video portion of my "Debt-Free/Stewardship" training for free as well. This allows them to network with us and, of course, helps them find deals via our network of investors. We have found that using the internet to capture leads for both investors and students is much more successful when we offer something for free in return for their information. After all, the more connections you have, the faster you're able to turn a property fast.

To sum up, we start our networking and marketing campaign as soon as the contract is signed. We let everyone know we have a deal, and that they need to act fast before someone else gets it. We also let them know that when they join our network, we can keep them updated on the latest deals and special events we have that they may want to be involved with.

One last thing: don't get so involved in the internet that you forget to get out in the field. When it comes to real estate investing, you need to be out there, touching, seeing and smelling real estate. I am an old-school investor, and started out being somewhat against all of this "do it online" stuff. Although I use the internet, it is only one tool. I am still out in the field regularly; something I require of my students as well. Once you're familiar with your market, you can spend more time on the computer. Just remember that the action is out in the field. It's where you can see the changes occurring or meet the nosey neighbor who can tell you everything about a property – who owns it, what happened to them, and even sometimes how to reach them. The internet can't do that! Yet.

Use the computer and the internet as tools to do research, to send out marketing campaigns and to build your reputation and company profile. Get out in the field to get to know and keep tabs on the changes in your market. This is how real estate investors find deals so they can get paid.

Getting Started

What next?

Now what? Well, first we have to formulate a plan based on every-thing we have learned so far. First, we must believe that we can make money in real estate. Then we have to decide if we are willing to get the training and knowledge needed to become successful, and get it now rather than someday. You see, someday never comes, so you must start now.

Mindset

You must train you mind. There's an old saying that if you think you can, or think you can't, you're right. The hardest obstacles to overcome are the self-defeating thoughts that occur in the six inches between your ears. You have to get your mind right in order to take positive action.

One of the best books I have found to get us into the right mindset is Napoleon Hill's *Think and Grow Rich*. By following the advice in his book, we can start training our mind to accomplish those things necessary to make our dreams come true. Other good ones you should read include: George S. Clason's *The Richest Man in Babylon*, Peter J. Daniels' *Miss Phillips, You Were Wrong: A Formula to Handle Rejection* and his *How to be Motivated All the Time,* and Laurie Beth Jones' *Jesus, CEO*. These books are designed to get your mind pointed in the right direction, and to guide you in conducting business with integrity while helping others and honoring God.

The absolutely best book to use as a guide for running your business from a biblical standpoint is Ed Silvoso's *Anointed for Business*. This will keep us focused on seeking and working for God. By doing business in a way that seeks first the Kingdom, we can then look at our gifts to see how we can use them to build our business. Now, this is very important: in my Debt Free training we learn that the business is really God's, not ours. Therefore we must build it on God's principles, not worldly principles. If we lay the foundation right and seek God and His will, then He can bless it.

Make a plan

Now that we have made up our minds that we can do it, and have set our focus correctly, we can start developing our business plans and setting our goals. We have to be able to do things for the new business every day, and if you work a full-time job, you have to be able to do that work after your job. Be sure not to sacrifice family time, and start each day with spending some quality time with God. A friend of mine learned it like this: God first, family second, career third. Only as an entrepreneur are you truly allowed to set and keep your priorities in this order, and isn't that how we all want our lives to be? By the way, you have to make career third, not thirty-third, or three hundred, because you'll never get to it then.

To give you an example, I normally work during the day. When the kids get out of school, I break and we do homework, karate, and family stuff. After dinner is over and the kids go to bed,

I may actually go back into my office to get some more work done. You need to realize that God has already given you all the time you are going to get. We all have 24 hours in day; the key is what you do with that time. I can tell you that I have been a bad steward of my time many, many times. However, the best thing to do is to set up a schedule and stick with it. Trust me, I know it can be tough, but it can be done. Try cutting out one television show, and you will be amazed at how much you can get done in that one hour. I am actually doing it myself right now as I write this chapter. You have to decide to make it happen, and then just do it!

Create a 30-day plan that includes everything you need to do to get your real estate career started. Day One will be to get some kind of daily planner, and write down one goal a day for thirty days to be done and completed. Perhaps on Day Two, you'll buy the books I mentioned, or get some training lined up that you might need to get the business going. Next, you should start building a power team of realtors, title companies, investors etc. One of those days you should use to track down a real estate club in your area, or find out where the nearest one is.

You should order some business cards so that when you network with other like-minded investors, you can give them your information and perhaps meet to discuss investing. You also need to keep records of all those contacts, so decide whether to use an address book or a computer program. It really doesn't matter what you use as long as you can quickly get to the information when you need it. You may also need to get something that allows you to have easy access but also integrate with how you will market. This may be a software-driven database or phone with built-in database ability that also works with your desktop.

I think you get the picture; we have to be moving forward every single day if we want to be successful in the real estate business, or any business for that matter. These thirty days' of goals are to be kept simple and small. What I mean is no huge goal, like buy a house in your first 30 days. You have to get through the learning curve, so to keep motivated, set small goals that must be accomplished each day. This way, our minds see that we are achieving the goals we have set out for ourselves. By keeping them small in the beginning, we do not set ourselves up for failure or discouragement if we immediately fail at the large goals.

Most people fail at being an entrepreneur because they set unrealistically huge goals in the very beginning without factoring in their learning curve. We all have a learning curve when we start something new, so we have to be able to learn what we need, how and when to apply the knowledge, and still get tasks and goals done. Setting small goals allows for a sense of accomplishment, and thus encourages us to keep moving forward.

We must make sure we see our 30-day goals every day. At the same time, we should mark off those things we've accomplished as they're completed. As we start to think ahead and make long-term goals such as one-year and five-year goals, remember to break them down into manageable chunks. These successive steps will end up being our 30-day goals which, over time, will result in reaching the long-term goals. Personally, I do not like to set any longer goals than five years out because there are too many things that can happen in that long of a period of time. We need to stay focused on the present, which will in turn get us paid sooner.

I want to suggest that you get a computer program to run all of your personal and business accounting; something like Microsoft Money or Quicken. You need to be able to run the business with ease and these programs allow you to handle all your banking and eventually can even run your rental properties. We have used very expensive property management programs in the past and found they were hard to use as well as very time consuming. Once we switched fully over to Microsoft Money, we were able to include the properties and eventually stopped using those expensive rental programs. I personally like Money because it is easy, capable of running property management and is very inexpensive. This will really help out when you get to end of year taxes and your CPA needs to see what all you have done in the new business; what properties you held and which ones you sold. By the way, as one of those first 30-day goals, get a CPA so they can help you structure your business.

For planning and goal setting, I like to use both a desk calendar and a wall calendar. The first thing I put on them are the Family days, i.e. birthdays, anniversaries, etc. We must put the priorities of life first, and that is God and family. This is why if I am ever doing training and it's on a Sunday, then we have a 20-minute church service in the classroom for the students who want to attend. I also want to make sure that family is first and those special dates stay special and remembered.

Next I put down the vacation days and real estate club meetings. The club dates are put down because this is part of what drives my business; a room full of investors, contractors, and everyone I work with in my business, all in one spot to network with. If you find yourself missing meetings, take a look at your business. I bet you will find it is not growing nor doing very well. I have always believed if you miss those things that can help you succeed on a regular basis, then your business will be tend to fail on a regular basis.

The wall calendar is used right next to my desk and can be seen from the whole office. It is color coded and lets me see the whole year at a glance. Above it, I have another wall calendar. This is the back of the previous year's calendar on which are the current year's top three goals for each of my businesses. This system works for me, but you need to find out what works for you.

Do not skip on something if you need it and it will make you more efficient. Sometimes, you end up spending more time, effort, and money trying to save $50. I am all about time and how valuable it is to want to waste it on being too cheap. In other words, don't trip over dollars to reach for the dimes. You have to realize you are starting a business, and there are certain costs associated with doing it. The reality is you are going to have to spend some money. Training costs money. Marketing costs money. Office supplies cost money. I'm not telling you to go out and buy everything you see; you must use your own judgment about what you truly need in order to run a successful business. However, if you don't get the proper training and tools, your cost is going to end up being much higher, because the true cost will end up being the unrealized success of your business.

Am I telling you to go into massive debt to start or operate your company? No, not at all. In fact, our goal is just the opposite. We need to be focused on God, and His will for our lives. He tells us to be a lender, not a borrower. Our goal is to keep our debt to a minimum as we build our business, and then to become debt-free personally and have only good debt (that which purchases the assets with cash flow) on the business side. Will you have to incur some short-term debt to get your company off the ground? I don't know; that depends on your unique financial situation. Some will, some won't. For those that do, one of your one-year goals is to pay that short-term debt off by successfully working your business and getting paid.

If you need help figuring out how to do this, I would like to suggest that you take my free online "Debt Free/Stewardship" training. The videos are free, but to get the most out of the program, you should purchase the accompanying workbook. Remember, time is the most important asset you have been given, so don't waste it by trying to recreate the book just to save a few dollars. Never forget that from here on out, you are a "three-percenter." Get the book, watch the videos, and get your business set up the right way.

I like to do things as though working with excellence for the Lord. I will be honest with you though; it was not always that way and I still occasionally find myself slipping to save a buck, especially when times are tough. This is when you need to take a moment from the situation and have a little quiet time with God. Ask Him to reveal His will in your prayer. Ask for guidance and peace on the situation. If you need to, take some time before you make the decision, but do not just put it off. If it seems like it would really help and you have prayed and have PEACE about it then do it.

I can tell you this; if you make a mistake, God will still take care of you. He will use the situation as a learning experience; I know – He has with me. By the way, I know this sounds like I have it all together – ha-ha! I blow it at least once day somewhere in my walk on this planet. Thank God He is full of mercy, grace, and love. With that knowledge, I continue on every day by remembering my favorite scripture, **Luke 9:23**. Instead of telling it to you here, I'd like you to look it up. My favorite part about using this verse in Luke is that it is the only Gospel where the word "daily" is used in the verse.

Ready, set, GO! Get started on your first 30-days goal sheet. Be realistic on what you can accomplish on a daily basis. Don't set Olympian goals for this time period, but don't just lie back and think it's all going to fall in your lap, either. Figure out how much time a day, a week you can commit to and stick to. Base your goals accordingly. Now that you have an idea of what you can accomplish in a month, you can start setting three-month, six-month and one-year goals.

Remember, all journeys start with the first step. As Will Rogers said, "Even if you're on the right track, you'll get run over if you just sit there." So get up right now, get a pen and a piece of paper, and get started!

Beginning Investors' Most Frequently Asked Questions

Typically you find FAQ at the back of an owner's manual of some sort. However, I wanted to add a chapter on the most frequently asked questions to the end of my book.

First, allow me to congratulate you on almost completing this book. I hope we've made it EASY enough for you. I also wanted to keep it short. I have a bad habit of not liking to read big books; in fact, I usually only buy thin books. I am more of a hands-on, visual type of learner. As such, I prefer watching a training video. I can see it, visually comprehend it and then watch it over and over until I really "Get It!"

I even do this is in my business here in Texas. I have weekend meetings with new and intermediate investors to try to locate and wholesale deals. We meet at a restaurant and discuss how, through networking together, we can all get paid. What has amazed me over the years is how over a period of about 6-8 weeks, the groups always dwindle down to just a few very motivated and serious investors.

You see, the Secret Formula or Technique everyone is always talking about that you need to succeed is really not what they are selling; it is actually the desire inside of you to succeed. In fact, if you have already read *Think and Grow Rich*, you will see that Chapter 2 in that book is titled "Desire." In Chapters 2 and 3, you will soon see what it takes to be an entrepreneur and a successful investor. No magic formulas or special scripts are necessary; it is simply the desire to make it happen and to have faith that it will happen until it actually does happen.

Now for these FAQ, I actually had a group I meet with a few Saturdays throughout the year help me come up with these questions. I thought, "what a way to see what new and intermediate investors need to know," based on what our group wanted to know. By the way, if you are following me on Twitter or YouTube, you will see that many times I say Team REED is doing something. Well, that is my group here in Fort Worth, Texas. Most of them attend our real estate club meeting once a month, but they needed and wanted more than that, and more importantly, they're willing to put forth the effort. I think our group is a great way to not only help them, but at the same time maybe we can all get some deals and get paid.

Therefore, I want to thank them first for being faithful at what they are trying to become in the real estate world; for always coming to the REIO-FW.com meetings; for always being at our Saturday meetings. It shows me that they are serious and that is what a seasoned investor in any market wants to do when networking. They want those who have that desire to make it. So Thank You, Team REED for the following questions for the final chapter of this book!

Question #1: How do I make it as an investor?

First, read *Think and Grow Rich* by Napoleon Hill, and then read it again to make sure you understand what you need to do as an investor. Make sure you have taken any training you need that will help you get on the fast track to success. One thing you definitely must do is remove yourself from being around negative people. At the very least, make sure they do not discourage you in regards to what you are trying to accomplish. I know so many people who have failed because their family and friends told them enough times that they would, so they believed it and that's exactly what happened; they failed. You must be in an environment that encourages your success and growth. It is one reason I suggest being in a real estate club or some kind of mastermind group. Here you can be with like-minded individuals with the same type of goals as you.

Question #2: When sending out postcards to owners of vacant properties, bail bondsmen, and for sale by owners, it is taking a long time to get any responses. What can I do to increase my calls?

Anytime you do a marketing campaign, you must have patience. A direct mail type of marketing campaign has to be done regularly with consistent tracking of responses. On average, it usually takes some-one receiving three of your marketing pieces before they actually see it. By the time you have sent something every two weeks for about eight weeks, they may have finally read it once.

To give you an example, in 1989, I started tracking a house next to a house I owned. I sent cards and letters for years with no responses. I even had other members on my team back then work that lead. It wasn't until 1998 that I gave the lead to a lady named Carmen. She did what no one else had ever done in those nine years; she actually drove to the owner's house and knocked on the door. Wow! No one, including me, took that extra step to make contact. A few hours later, she emerged from his house with the property under contract. It wasn't even all cash; it was owner financed with only $2,000 down.

You see, she had a "three-percenter" attitude to succeed. Remember this while you are marketing. Needless to say, we got a fantastic deal and no bank needed. You have to persistently work it consistently, and sometimes get out of the BOX! The old formula goes like this:

Consistency x Persistence = Success!

Question #3: How do I market using the internet?

If you already have a webpage, of course you start and build around that. However, if you are on a budget, I suggest you get the book *Secrets of Social Media Marketing*. This can guide you on how to implement marketing strategies to reach the goals you have planned out. My goals may be different than yours but there are some basic similarities. Start with setting up some type of free networking forum on the internet. I like YouTube and would suggest creating a free YouTube channel. It is really easy and besides, most folks today want videos over any other application of communication. You can get a video camera with really good features starting at around $100. Then you make some videos and upload them to the world.

You also need to learn what tag words motivated sellers are searching with. This is probably the hardest part. Pretend you're the motivated seller – type in the words you would search with if you had to sell your house. See what key words come up and then use them.

Next, you should look at Craigslist and eBay for folks trying to sell a property. You can try this out and see what you think. A lot of my students have had success with it; I personally have not. I like building my network and doing the kind of marketing that lets folks know that "I BUY HOUSES; contact me if you need CASH!" I use Twitter and LinkedIn for some real major marketing. Many people use them. These sites not only help you find some motivated sellers, but can also build your database of investors who are buying. Remember, when using the internet you reach the world market, not just your local one.

Lastly, try using Facebook. It is one of the most popular social networks. Whether you are looking for an investor, a seller, or a plumber, everyone is rushing to set up a Facebook account, so get one now! Keep in mind, all of this builds your network and all of it is free (at least, at the time of this writing it is). Eventually you want all these spider networks to link back to your webpage. This is one of those tools we talked about earlier that you need to get as soon as you can afford it. You can look at mine and see how I have had it designed to meet several needs, from buying and selling properties, to training, to helping folks become debt free. Check it out again at www.JimmyReed.net.

Question #4: Why do I have to be pre-qualified when I'm making offers through a realtor?

Oh boy, the ole "making offers through a realtor to **NON**-Motivated Sellers," and right now, that tends to be the bank! I tell my students all the time I know that short sales and foreclosures are popular, but stop and think. The reason those owners are currently in foreclosure in this market is because they all owe more than what the property is worth. The banks are not motivated to cut deals because we (the taxpayers) have bailed them out. Therefore, they are not motivated, and thus insist you play by their rules.

My number one rule is to always have a Motivated Seller; if they are not truly motivated, move on! Don't get me wrong; a lot of successful investors in today's market love to do short sales. I, however, do not. I like a deal now, not three months down the road and only after processing tons of paperwork. I will take a vacant, boarded-up, probate estate, or plain ol' motivated seller before I spend that much time doing short sales. Besides, you cannot assign a short sale; you usually have to do a double close which is fine. But again, it's their rules. They typically want a pre-qualification letter and $1,000 earnest money. Two weeks after you've made your offer, they respond with "we need your best offer now since we have several and we are going to pick one in the morning." Yeah, whatever!

If the government wants to do something right to stabilize the housing market, then they should bring back the RTC. Let them strip the assets from troubled banks and sell them to investors cheaply for cash, like they did in the late '80s and early '90s. That will stimulate the economy. You will have so many properties selling to investors every day that those investors will be hiring contractors and getting title companies busy doing closings. Another option would be for mortgage companies to underwrite loans, and then have realtors sell them for 15% below what they were three years earlier; then everyone, including the homeowner, WINS!

For now, go find a deal and stop wasting your time with the banks. The fact is if every investor would stop jumping through those hoops and stop making those offers, guess what might happen to the banks? They may actually wake up and get motivated, especially if we stop bailing them out. What do you think; are you in for the boycott?

Question #5: Why do some realtors refuse to work with you when you make really low offers?

I hate to say it, but you have the wrong realtor, and there are plenty of them out there. Remember, they are paid on commission. They know if your offer is close to what the seller wants, it might get accepted. However, most of them are kind of like the banks; they're not motivated to represent an offer for less than ARV.

Over the years, I have learned how to find the right type of realtors. They are the ones who are investors themselves; they have rehabbed properties and managed them. You need one who understands that an investor might be making low offers, but that same investor is also a repeat buyer. They need to know volume over time outweighs the one-time homeowner who will pay a retail price. Realtors generally list houses by sellers who want as much as they can possibly get. On the other hand, truly motivated sellers have to sell the property yesterday in "as is" condition for all cash. Well guess what? More than likely, the buyer of that property is going to be an investor.

I'll let you in on a little secret; some of the best realtors can be found at your local real estate investor club. Over the years, I have had investors fly in or drive in to our club to see how it works, make contacts, and then head back to their state and do the same thing. You see, there are a lot of real estate clubs, but not all of them are designed as investor-friendly clubs. Investor-friendly clubs are more about the networking, flipping deals, and building a power team. That is the kind of club a seasoned investor wants to attend to build his business! With this in mind, get to a club and find a motivated realtor.

Question #6: Are bad foundations and major rehabs worth the time and effort?

Yes, yes, yes! This is where you have an opportunity to get the absolutely best price. In this instance, there are no homeowners trying to compete and drive up the price. Most people do not want really bad properties. However, if you can get them far enough below retail price, you have a chance to make some serious cash.

In fact, my personal home is the perfect example. Our house sat on the market for two years, had sold three times and never funded. You see, it was in terrible shape. It had foundation problems; 23 piers to be exact. It needed a brand new roof with new decking. It had a sign on the front door from HUD that said "presence of mold."ABthat will scare potential buyers away! The pool looked like the septic tank, and the kitchen was falling apart. Other than that, it was great! What I liked is it's a nearly 3,300 sq.ft, 4-5-3 on nearly 3 acres, 15 minutes outside the city. The comps at the time we purchased it were nearly $350,000–$400,000.

The best part was that because of all the mold, no one could get financing on it. For two years the price kept on dropping until an investor friend of mine, Tim, told me about it. I made my offer, and a week later after we thought they had not accepted, we found out we were the proud owners of this dump. The real kicker is we only paid $115,000. It cost us $65,000 to do the rehab including going $14,000 over budget on our pool. It could have been done for $3,000, but oh well, it is our home. Now do the math on it and look at how much equity we have in it. In fact, I am doing a HELOC on it for about $200,000 as I write this book. We can do this because we have owned it free and clear since the year after we purchased it. By the way, I think my next book will tell you how four rentals paid off our home, but that's in the next book. Basically, YES, bad conditions can equal big bucks!

Question #7: What are the best ways to market to investors who can pay cash and close quickly?

You can always find them if you have a really great deal. Simply put, most serious cash buyers are always looking in the newspapers, shoppers' guides and driving the neighborhoods that they like to buy in. You need to put up a sign on the property you have for sale the minute you put it under contract. Then run an ad immediately in the newspaper and local shoppers' guides. Print up some flyers and distribute them at the local investor club and the neighborhood where the property is located. Then call all the other "I Buy Houses" investors in those same newspapers.

Grab any and all info at your club; usually it's on a deal table of some sort. Make sure to introduce yourself to the club owners or leaders and see if they can introduce you to the major players in the club. You can also run ads in out-of-state markets where real estate is very expensive. This gets the attention of investors who want to buy at better price points than their home markets, such California, New York, Chicago; you get the point. Find the deal and they will come!

Question #8: How do I find Private Money Lenders?

You use the same strategies as finding cash investors, but your focus will be on the clubs and the newspaper. This time you are looking for ads that say "Money to Lend." You can find many hard money lenders as well as investors who want to get a better return on their investment than they would at their local bank in a CD or stock.

You may also be surprised to find that you have a friend or family member who might want a better return by investing their money in your deal than they are getting now. My Grandmother was my first money lender when I first got started. I could pay her more than the 6-8% she was getting in her CD's so she invested with me. Of course, grandmas tend to be willing to take a little more risk with their grandchildren then someone else would. My grandmother was kind of tough, too. If we did not get the deal done right, she would say "we gonna be equity owners real soon if you do not get it turned." This would have been fine with me. She would actually say "It's Gonna be All Riiiiiight!"

Question #9: What if we can't get rid of the property?

This is very simple; you use your escape clause. You must start each deal the right way, inserting your "and/or assigns," and most of all the "subject to inspections and partners' approvals" provision. You always have your exit door ready to open and leave if needed. Let the seller know that "it looks like this deal is just not going to work for me and my partners." The fact is you told them up front while putting the property under contract that if it did not meet your requirements, you would walk away. That is what you do. Send a letter to both the title company and the seller, letting them know you have decided not to move forward with the transaction.

Congratulations! You have made it to the end, and I want to add this little encouragement for you. When I first started out, I was trying to make this work for over nine months before I finally got paid. I backed out of a lot of contracts in that time. I also made a lot of offers to be able to back out a lot of times. The key to your success is never, never, never give up! You must do as Sir Winston Churchill said which, by the way I actually have this hanging on my office wall, is "**Perseverance** – *Continuous effort is the key to unlocking our potential.*" If you approach life with this concept, you will succeed. I wish you all the best. Make sure you are a part of my network at www.JimmyReed.net and check out some of our trainings that may help you increase the speed of your success. We also want you to take our free debt free/stewardship training online, but make sure you get the book; it will make it easier and faster to complete.

Remember always that time is the most valuable asset you have been given. Spend it with God, family, and loved ones. Do what you can to make life better for others and try using this little question to help better yourself and others:

When you are gone one day, what will be the God-given gift that everyone you know will miss?

Glossary

Abandon - To choose not to exercise or sell an option before it expires. To voluntarily relinquish the rights of property ownership.

Abstract (of Title) - A historical summary of all the recorded transactions that affect the title to the property. An attorney or a title company will review an abstract of title to determine if there are any problems affecting the title to the property. All such problems must be cleared before the buyer can be issued a clear and insurable title.

Acceleration Clause - A provision in a loan contract that allows the lender to demand full and immediate repayment of the entire loan balance if the contract is breached or conditions for repayment occur.

Addendum - Clauses that are added to the end of a contract which supersede what is written in the contract.

Adjustable Rate Mortgage (ARM) - Also known as a variable rate mortgage. A mortgage with an interest rate that may change, usually in response to changes in the Treasury Bill rate or the prime rate.

Agent - Generally, someone who acts on behalf of another for a fee. In real estate, the term refers to a person with a real estate license who works under the authority of a real estate broker.

Agreement of Sale - A written signed agreement between the seller and the purchaser in which the purchaser agrees to buy certain real estate and the seller agrees to sell upon terms of the agreement. Also known as contract of purchase, purchase agreement, offer and acceptance, earnest money contract or sales agreement.

Amortization - A gradual paying off of a debt by regular periodic installments which pay principal and interest over a specified period of time.

Annual Percentage Rate (APR) - The effective rate of interest for a loan per year. This rate is typically higher than the note rate because it takes into account closing costs. This is one way to compare loan programs offered by different lenders. Caution: the APR is sometimes computed differently by different lenders and can be misleading.

Appraisal - An opinion or estimate of the value of a property at a given date.

Appreciation - Increase in value of a property.

Arm's Length Transaction - Typically, a transaction between two related or affiliated parties that is conducted as if they were unrelated, so that there is no question of a conflict of interest.

Arrears - The amount of debt that is overdue or unpaid. A payment that is made past its due date.

Assessment - A local tax levied against a property for a specific purpose such as street lights.

Asset - Anything of value can be converted into cash or used to pay a debt.

Assign - To transfer interest.

Assignee - Individual to whom a title, claim, property, interest, or right has been transferred.

Assignor - The one who transfers a title, claim, property, interest, or right to another person.

Assignment Clause - A sales contract with an assignment clause allows the buyer to transfer the interest in the property (e.g. the right to buy it at the given rates and terms) to another party.

Assumable Mortgage - A mortgage loan which allows a new home buyer to take over the obligation of making loan payments with no change in the terms of the loan. Assumable loans do not have a due-on-sale clause. The lender has to be notified and agree to the assumption. The lender may require the buyer to qualify for the loan and may charge an assumption fee. The seller should obtain a written release from the lender stating clearly that he/she is no longer liable to make mortgage payments. See also "Subject To".

Assumption - To assume a mortgage means to take over the repaying of that debt from the seller.

Balloon (payment) Mortgage - Usually a short-term fixed-rate loan which involves small payments for a certain period of time and one large payment for the remaining amount of the principal at a time specified in the contract. Example: A balloon mortgage for $25,000 has interest only payments for 5 years at 12% ($250 per month), with the full principal of $25,000 due and payable after 5 years.

Bankruptcy - The financial inability to pay one's debts when due. The debtor surrenders his assets to the bankruptcy court. An individual typically files for Chapter 7 (all debts wiped out) or Chapter 13 (establishes a payment plan to pay off debts). A bankruptcy stays on an individual's credit report for 7 years.

Beneficiary - The person who receives or is eligible to receive the benefits resulting from certain acts. If you set up a land trust for a property that you own, you are the beneficiary.

Bid - An offer of a specific amount of money in exchange for products and services, as in an auction.

Bi-weekly Mortgage - A mortgage which requires 1/2 the normal monthly payment every two weeks. Over the course of the year, 26 half-payments are made which is equivalent to 13 full mortgage payments. As a result of this extra payment, the loan amortizes much faster than a loan with normal monthly payments.

Blanket Mortgage - A mortgage covering more than one piece of property. Example: A developer subdivides a tract of land into lots and obtains a blanket mortgage on the whole tract.

Borrower (Mortgagor) - One who applies for a loan secured by real estate and is responsible for repaying the loan (mortgage).

Broker - An individual or firm which acts as an intermediary between a buyer and seller, usually charging a commission.

Buy-Back Agreement - An agreement specifying conditions under which the seller agrees to repurchase the property, usually for a stated price and within a stated time limit.

Buy Down - Obtaining a lower interest rate (buying down the rate) by paying additional points to the lender. The lower rate may apply for the full duration of the loan or for just the first few years. A buy down may be used to qualify a borrower who would otherwise not qualify. This is because a buy down results in lower payments which are easier to qualify for. Example: A very popular buy down is the 2-1 buy down. If the interest rate on the note is 9%, the buy down results in the rate being 7% (9%-2%) for the first year, 8% (9%-1%) for the second year, and 9% thereafter.

Buyers Broker - An agent hired by a buyer to locate a property for purchase. The broker represents the buyer and negotiates with the seller's broker for the best possible deal for the buyer.

Buyers Market - Market conditions that favor buyers i.e. there are more sellers than buyers in the market. As a result buyers have ample choice of properties and may negotiate lower prices. Buyers markets may be caused by an economic slump or overbuilding.

Capital - Money used to generate income.

Capital Gains - Profit earned from the sale of real estate or the amount by which an asset's selling price exceeds its initial purchase price. A seller may defer taxes on the capital gain of his/her primary residence by buying a higher priced residence within 2 years.

Capitalization Rate - The rate used to determine the present value of property with future earnings.

CAPS (interest) - Consumer safeguards which limit the amount the interest rate on an adjustable rate mortgage may change per year and/or over the life of the loan.

CAPS (payment) - Consumer safeguards which limit the amount monthly payments on an adjustable rate mortgage may change.

Cash Flow - The amount of cash derived over a certain period of time from an income-producing property. Cash receipts minus cash payments over a given period of time. The cash flow should be large enough to pay the expenses of the income-producing property (mortgage payment, maintenance, utilities, etc.).

Certificate of Occupancy - Document issued by a local governmental agency that states a property meets the local building standards for occupancy and is in compliance with public health and building codes. This document is normally required by a lender prior to closing the loan.

Certificate of Title - An opinion rendered by an attorney as to the status of title to a property, according to the public records. This certificate does not hold the same level of protection as title insurance.

Chain of Title - Chronological order of conveyance of a parcel of land from the original owner to the present owner. An abstractor can research title to property going back to the date that the property was granted to the United States.

Clear Title - A marketable title, free of liens and legal questions as to the ownership of the property. Most lenders require a clear title prior to closing.

Closing - 1. The act of transferring ownership of a property from seller to buyer in accordance with a sales contract. 2. The time when a closing takes place. 3. The process of signing the documents to transfer property.

Closing Costs - Expenses incurred by the buyer and seller in a real estate or mortgage transaction over and above the price of the property. There are two types of costs: recurring and non-recurring. Non-recurring costs are one-time transactional costs, which include: Discount and origination points, Lender fees - underwriting, processing, document preparations, flood certificate, tax service, wire transfer, courier, etc. Title insurance fees, Escrow, attorney or closing agent fees, Recording fees, Inspection and appraisal fees, and Real estate brokerage commissions. Recurring fees are costs associated with owning the property and they recur month after month. These costs may include hazard insurance, interest, property taxes, mortgage insurance (PMI), and association fees. A pro-rated amount of these fees may have to be paid at closing including Pre-paid interest - interest charges from the date of closing to the end of the month, Property taxes if due, Hazard insurance, fire insurance or homeowner's insurance has to be paid for one year. Mortgage insurance (PMI) - may be required if the loan amount is more than 80% of the value of the property. In the past a whole year of PMI had to be paid up front, however in recent years many PMI companies only require 1-2 months up front. Mortgage insurance premiums are normally paid every month with the loan payment Impound account may need money to be set up for future payments

Closing Statement - The settlement statement that discloses all of the financial information of the transaction for the buyer and seller including all costs.

Cloud on Title - An outstanding claim or encumbrance that, if valid, would affect or impair the owner's title. Compared with clear title.

Collateral - Assets pledged by a borrower to secure a loan or other credit, and subject to seizure in the event of default.

Commission - The fee charged by a broker or agent when selling real estate.

Comparative Market Analysis (CMA) - A comparison of sales prices of similar properties in a given area for the purpose of determining the fair market value of a property. Also referred to as "Comps."

Consideration - Anything of value given to induce another to enter into a contract. Earnest money deposit on a sales contract is consideration.

Construction Loan - A short term loan to pay for the construction of buildings or homes. These loans typically provide periodic disbursements to the builder as each stage of the building is completed. When construction is completed a "take-out" or permanent loan is used to pay off the construction loan.

Contingency - Conditions which must be satisfied before the buyer can close the purchase of a property. Contingencies are generally outlined in the purchase contract between the buyer and seller. Example: The buyer has 14 days to remove the property contingency under the sales contract. In this case the buyer has 14 days to inspect the property and request the seller to perform repairs. If the buyer is not satisfied with the condition of the property or if the buyer and the seller cannot agree on repairs, the buyer may back out of the contract with no penalty. After 14 days the buyer no longer has the right to back out with no penalty as a result of a problem with the condition of the property.

Contract - A binding agreement between competent parties to do or not do certain things for consideration. To have a valid contract for the sale of real estate there must be: 1) an offer, 2) an acceptance, 3) competent parties, 4) consideration, 5) legal purpose, 6) written documentation, 7) description of the property, 8) signatures by principals or their attorney-in-fact.

Contract of Sale - Same as the Agreement of Sale

Contract Sale or Deed - A real estate installment selling arrangement where the buyer may occupy the property but the seller retains the title until the agreed upon sales price has been paid. Also known as an installment land contract.

Contract to Purchase - An agreement of sale detailing the transaction and submitted by the buyer to the seller.

Conventional Loan - Any mortgage loan other than a VA or an FHA loan. A conventional loan may be conforming or non-conforming.

Conveyance - The transfer of title of real property from one party to another.

Co-op - A multi-unit housing complex where the residents own stock in the building instead of individual units.

Corporation - An association of one or more shareholders having its own legal entity separate from the individual shareholders.

Covenant - A written agreement or restriction on the use of land or promising certain acts. Homeowner Associations often enforce restrictive covenants governing architectural controls and maintenance responsibilities. However, land could be subject to restrictive covenants even if there is no homeowner's association.

Credit Report - A report detailing a borrower's credit history including payment history on revolving accounts (e.g. credit cards), installment accounts (e.g. car loan), bankruptcies and late payments, and recent inquiries. It can be obtained by prospective lenders with the borrower's permission, to determine his or her creditworthiness. A credit report also includes information found from public records including tax liens and judgments.

Debt-to-Income Ratio - The ratio, expressed as a percentage, which results when a borrower's monthly payment obligation on long-term debts is divided by his or her net effective income (FHA/VA loans) or gross monthly income (conventional loans).

Deed - A written document by which title to real property is transferred from one owner to another. The deed should contain an accurate description of the property being conveyed, should be signed and witnessed according to the laws of the State where the property is located, and should be delivered to the buyer at closing.

Deed of Trust - Used in many states instead of a mortgage to secure the payment of a note. In a deed of trust there are three parties - the borrower, the trustee, and the lender, (or beneficiary). The deed to a property is held by a trustee instead of the borrower.

Deed Restriction - A clause in a deed that limits the use of land. Example: A deed might require that a road cannot be built on the land.

Default - Failure to meet legal obligations in a contract - such as the failure to make the monthly mortgage payment.

Defective Title - Any recorded instrument that would prevent a grantor/seller from giving a clear title. Example: The seller has a contractor lien on the property that was filed when he/she failed to pay the contractor for the kitchen remodel. The seller may obtain clear title by paying the contractor and removing the lien.

Delinquency - Failure to make payments on time. This can lead to foreclosure.

Depreciation - Decline in the value of a house due to wear and tear, obsolescence, adverse changes in the neighborhood, or any other reason.

Disclosure - Statement of fact(s) concerning the condition of the property for sale and the surrounding area. In most states, the buyer is protected by disclosure laws requiring sellers to divulge certain information about the property, e.g. if the property is in a special studies zone.

Discount Points - Fees paid to a lender to reduce the interest rate.

Down Payment - The part of the purchase price paid in cash up front, reducing the amount of the loan or mortgage. Example: John buys a house for $100,000 and obtains a loan for $80,000. His down payment is $20,000.

Due on Sale Clause - A clause in the Deed of Trust or Mortgage that states that the entire loan is due upon the sale of the property.

Earnest Money - A deposit made by a buyer of real estate towards the down payment to evidence good faith. This money is typically held by the real estate broker or the escrow company.

Easement - The right to use the land of another for a specific purpose. Easements may be temporary or permanent. Example: The utility company may need an easement to run electric lines.

Eminent Domain - The right of the government or a public utility to acquire private property for public use by condemnation, with proper compensation to the owner.

Encumbrance - A legal right or interest in land that affects a good or clear title, and diminishes the land's value. It can take numerous forms, such as zoning ordinances, easement rights, claims, mortgages, liens, charges, a pending legal action, unpaid taxes, or restrictive covenants. An encumbrance does not legally prevent transfer of the property to another. A title search is all that is usually done to reveal the existence of such encumbrances, and it is up to the buyer to determine whether he wants to purchase with the encumbrance, or what can be done to remove it.

Equal Credit Opportunity Act (ECOA) - A federal law that requires lenders and other creditors to make credit equally available without discrimination based on race, color, religion, national origin, age, sex, marital status or receipt of income from public assistance programs.

Equity (Equity=Property Value - Loans/Liens Against the property) - The property value minus what you still owe (the mortgage balance).

Escrow - An account held by the lender into which a homeowner pays money for taxes and insurance

Eviction - The lawful removal of an occupant and her/his belongings from a property.

Fannie Mae/Federal National Mortgage Association (FNMA) - Purchases loans from lenders then sells them as FNMA mortgage backed securities on Wall Street.

Farmer's Home Administration (FmHA) - An agency, within the U.S. Department of Agriculture, that makes and insures loans for rural housing and farms.

Federal Deposit Insurance Corporation (FDIC) - A government agency that supervises and insures accounts.

Fee Simple (Fee Absolute or Fee Simple Absolute) - Absolute ownership of real property; owner is entitled to the entire property with unrestricted power of disposition during the owners life and upon his death the property descends to the owner's designated heirs.

Federal Housing Administration (FHA) - A government agency within HUD that administers and insures mortgage loans for private lending agencies.

FHA Loan - This program provides mortgage insurance to protect lenders against the risk of default on loans to qualified buyers. A loan insured by the Federal Housing Administration is open to all qualified home purchasers. The FHA does not make loans to borrowers, it does not process loans and it does not build or insure houses. While there are limits to the size of FHA loans, they are generous enough to handle moderately-priced homes almost anywhere in the country.

FICO Score - FICO stands for Fair Isaac & Company. Credit scores are reported by three major credit bureaus, Equifax, Experian and Trans-Union. Scores are not the same on each bureau's report because each bureau places a slightly different value on different items. Scores may range from 364 to 840.

Fiduciary - A person in a position of trust or responsibility with the legal authority and duty to make decisions regarding financial matters on behalf of the other party. A real estate broker is a fiduciary for his/her clients.

Finance Charge - Interest charged by a lender.

Fixed Rate Mortgage (FRM) - The mortgage interest rate will remain the same throughout the term of the mortgage for the original borrower.

Forbearance - A lenders postponement of foreclosure in order to give the borrower time and an opportunity to make up for overdue payments.

Foreclosure (Repossession) - A legal sale of property forced by the lender when the borrower defaults on the mortgage loan.

Freddie Mac/Federal Home Loan Mortgage Corporation (FHLMC) - Purchases loans from the Federal Reserve and the Federal Home Loan Bank Systems then sells them as FHLMC mortgage backed securities on Wall Street.

Free and Clear - A property that has no liens. See also "Clear Title."

FSBO (For Sale by Owner) - A property for sale that is not listed with a real estate broker and therefore will not be listed on the Multiple Listing Service (MLS).

Grace Period - The time period between the due date of a mortgage payment and the date when late charges are assessed. For example, payments due on the first of the month may have a 14 day grace period, meaning that fees will be charged if payment is not received by the fifteenth.

Graduated Payment Mortgage (GPM) - A mortgage that has lower payments initially (with potential negative amortization) which increase each year until the loan is fully amortized. Intended for young people with low current income but greater anticipated future income.

Grantee - That party in the deed who is the buyer or recipient.

Grantor - That party who is the seller or the giver.

Hard Money Lender - Lenders who use private money to make loans with Borrowers who have trouble getting loans via conventional methods. There is usually a very high interest rate associated with hard money lenders.

Home-Improvement Loan - A loan used to finance home improvements. It may or may not require a mortgage or collateral.

Homeowner's Association - An association of homeowners that oversees the common areas of the development and its rules and regulations.

Home Warranty Plan - Private insurance insuring a buyer against defects (usually in plumbing, electrical, appliances and heating systems. Typically purchased at the time of closing and can cover both new and used homes.

Homestead - Status provided to a homeowner's principal residence in some states that protects the home against judgments up to specified amounts.

Homestead Exemption - Available in some states - this causes the assessed value of a principal residence to be reduced by the amount of the exemption for the purposes of calculating property tax.

Housing and Urban Development (HUD) - A U.S. government agency established to implement certain federal housing and community development programs.

Improvements - Additions to raw land such as buildings, streets, etc. that add value to the land.

Income Approach - A method used by an appraiser to estimate the value of rental property based on the income it generates over the life of the structure, discounted to determine its present value.

Income Property - Real estate that generates rental income.

Ingress and Egress - The right to go in and out over a piece of property but not the right to park on it. See also Easements.

Inspection - An examination of a property or building to determine condition or quality for a particular purpose such as an assessment of structural or termite damage. Also to confirm that the property meets the standards of the contract.

Installment Sale - See land contract.

Interest Cap - A limit on the amount that the interest rate for an adjustable rate mortgage can change, regardless of how much the index changes. Most ARMs have a cap on either the amount it can increase or decrease at any periodic adjustment interval and a life-long cap that limits the amount the interest rate can vary over the life of the loan. The two interest caps are sometimes called a "periodic cap" and a "life cap".

Interest rate - The percentage rate on a principal amount charged by a lender for the use of a sum of money.

Investor - A money source for a lender. Also, one who makes investments.

Junior Lien - When a property is foreclosed, lenders are repaid in a particular order, established by the loan documents. The lender with the first claim to repayment is said to hold the first mortgage, and a lender whose repayment order is after the first claimant is said to hold a junior, or subordinate lien.

Junior Mortgage - All mortgages/liens subordinate to the first mortgage. In the case of a foreclosure a senior mortgage will be paid prior to a junior mortgage.

Land Contract - A real estate installment selling arrangement whereby the buyer may use and occupy land, but ownership of the property is not transferred until all the payments have been made.

Landlord - The owner of real property who rents or leases to another party, called a tenant.

Land Trust - Used to protect your assets (your property). Only the Trustee is named in public records; you, the Beneficiary, are not named.

Lease - An agreement giving the right to occupy property for a specific period of time for a specific amount.

Lease Option - An agreement giving the renter has the option to purchase the property.

Lease with Option to Purchase - A lease under which the lessee has the right to purchase the property. The option may run for a portion or for the full length of the lease

Lessee - A person leases a property from its owner. (Tenant)

Lessor - A person who rents property to another under a lease. (Landlord)

Lien - A claim against the property for the payment of a debt, judgment, mortgage or taxes. A lien must be satisfied when the property is sold. Example: Unpaid contractors may file a mechanic's lien.

Lis Pendens - "Lawsuit Pending"

Loan Application - A document required by a lender prior to loan approval. The application includes detailed information about the borrower, their finances, and the property.

Loan Origination Fee or Points - A one-time fee charged by a lender or broker connected with originating a loan. This is different from discount points which are used to buy down the rate of interest.

Loan-to-Value Ratio (LTV) - The relationship of the loan amount to the price (or value) of the property.

Manufactured Home - Homes built in a factory-controlled environment and meet the strict HUD codes. They are brought to the property site and are assembled there.

Margin - A fixed number added to the index to compute the rate on an adjustable rate mortgage.

Market Value - The highest price that a buyer would pay and the lowest price a seller would accept on a property. Market value may be different from the price a property could actually be sold for at a given time.

Mortgage - A written legal agreement that creates a lien against a property as security for the payment of a debt; a loan to pay for real estate that usually includes interest rates and a payment schedule.

Mortgage Banker - Specializes in originating, selling and servicing loans. They generally sell their loans to investors, but may continue to service them.

Mortgage Broker - An individual or company which brings borrowers and lenders together for the purpose of loan origination, but which does not originate or service the mortgages. They are paid a fee by the borrower or the seller at the closing.

Mortgagee - The lender.

Mortgagor - The borrower.

Motivated Buyer - Any buyer with a strong circumstance or reason to buy.

Motivated Seller - Any seller with a strong circumstance or reason to sell.

Multiple Listing Service (MLS) - A group of brokers joined together in a marketing organization for the purpose of pooling their respective listings. In exchange for a potentially larger audience of buyers, the brokers agree to share commissions. The listings are pooled by using a computerized network.

Negative Amortization - An increase in principal balance which occurs when the monthly payments do not cover all of the interest cost. The interest cost which is not covered by the payment is added to the unpaid principal balance.

Net Operating Income (NOI) - The amount of income you have left after you deduct operating expenses (but before deducting interest and taxes). NOI does not include debt service (mortgage payment).

Non-Assumption Clause - A statement in a mortgage contract forbidding the assumption of the mortgage without the prior approval of the lender.

Noncompliance - Failure to comply or obey.

Non-Conforming Loan - A loan that does not meet the Freddie Mac or Fannie Mae standards.

Notary Public - One authorized to take acknowledgments of certain types of documents, such as deeds, contracts, and mortgages.

Note - A legal document that obligates a borrower to repay a mortgage loan at a specified interest rate during a specified period of time or on demand.

Notice of Default - A formal notice to a borrower declaring that a default has occurred and that legal action may be taken.

Offer - An expression of willingness to purchase a property at a specified price.

Option - The right to buy a property at a specific price within a specific time period.

Optionee - One who receives or purchases an option.

Optionor - One who gives or sells an option.

Option to Purchase - An agreement giving the right to buy a property at a specific price within a specific time period.

Oral Contract - A verbal agreement. Verbal agreements for the sale or use of real estate are normally unenforceable.

Origination Fee - A fee charged by a lender for processing a loan application, expressed as a percentage of the mortgage amount.

Owner Occupant - A tenant of a residence who also owns the property.

Owner of Record - The individual named on a deed that has been recorded at the county recorder's office.

Paper - A mortgage, deed of trust or land contract provided in lieu of cash.

PITI - Abbreviation for principal, interest, taxes and insurance, which may be combined in a single monthly mortgage payment.

Plat - A plan or map of a specific land area.

Plat Book - A public record containing maps of land, showing the division of the land into streets, blocks, and lots and indicating the measurements of the individual parcels.

Points - Fees paid to lenders at the beginning of a loan. 1 point=1% of the loan amount. On a $100,000 loan 1 point is $1000. Points may be further classified into origination points or discount points.

Portfolio Loan - A loan held (not sold) by banks as an investment.

Power of Attorney - A written document authorizing another to act on his or her behalf and is called an Attorney in Fact. One does not need to be a licensed attorney to act as an attorney in fact but, power of attorney forms are powerful legal documents that should be used only under advice of a licensed attorney at law.

Prepaid Interest - Interest paid before it is earned. Prepaid interest is the interest charged to borrowers at closing to pay for the cost of borrowing for a balance of the month. For example, if a loan closes on the 19th of the month and the first payment is due on the 1st of the following month, the lender will charge 12 days of prepaid interest.

Prepayment - Full or partial payment of the principal before the due date. This might occur if the borrower makes extra payments, sells the property, or refinances the existing loan.

Prime Rate - The lowest commercial interest rate charged by a bank on short term loans to their most credit worthy customers.

Principal - The outstanding balance on a loan.

Private Mortgage Insurance (PMI) - Mortgage insurance provided by non-government insurers that protects a lender against loss if the borrower defaults. In the event the borrower doesn't have a 20 percent down payment, lenders will allow a smaller down payment - as low as 2 percent in some cases. With the smaller down payment loans, however, borrowers are usually required to carry private mortgage insurance. Private mortgage insurance payments are normally made annual or monthly.

Probate - Court process to establish the validity of the will of a deceased person. Also, the process by which an executor (if there is a will) or a court-appointed administrator (if there is not a will) manages and distributes a decedent's property.

Pro Forma - Projected financial statements based on assumptions.

Promissory Note - A signed legal document that acknowledges the existence of a debt and the promise to repay it.

Prorate - To divide proportionately, so as to determine actual amounts owed by the buyer and seller at closing. For example, if property taxes for a month are $300 and the seller owned the property for the first 10 days while the borrower owned the property for the remaining 20 days, the property taxes owed would be prorated so that the seller would pay $100 ($300 * 10/30) and the buyer would pay $200 ($300 * 20/30).

Public Sale - An auction of property that is open to the general public. A public sale generally requires notice (advertising) and must be held in a place accessible to the general public.

Purchase - To buy; or, to obtain property in exchange for money.

Purchase Agreement - See Agreement of Sale.

Purchase Money Mortgage - A mortgage used to finance the purchase of a property.

Qualifying - The process of determining whether a buyer is financially able to assume a mortgage by checking credit history, present and previous employment, and any other sources which may help to determine the buyer's financial capability.

Quit Claim Deed - A deed which transfers whatever interest or title the maker of the deed may have in the particular parcel of land. A quitclaim deed is often given to clear the title when the grantor's interest in a property is questionable. By accepting such a deed, the buyer assumes all the risk. Such a deed makes no warranties as to the title, but simply transfers to the buyer whatever interest the grantor has.

Real Estate Broker - A licensed individual who arranges the buying and selling of real estate for a fee. A broker usually owns his own real estate company or is in a management position.

Real Property - Land including trees, minerals, and any permanent fixtures attached to it.

Realtor - A real estate professional who is a member of the National Association of Realtors.

Recording - The act of entering into a book of public records instruments affecting title to the real property. A lender requires that a deed of trust or a mortgage be recorded to evidence the debt against the property.

Recording Fees - Money paid to the lender for recording a home sale with the local authorities, thereby making it part of the public records.

Red-Lining - Illegal practice of discriminating based on geographic location when providing loans or insurance coverage.

Refinance - Obtaining a new mortgage loan on a property already owned. Often to replace existing loans on the property.

Refinancing - Repaying an existing loan from the proceeds of a new loan on the same property.

Restrictive Covenants - Private restrictions limiting the use of real property. Restrictive covenants are created by deed and may "run with the land," binding all subsequent purchasers of the land, or may be "personal" and binding only between the original seller and buyer.

Right of First Refusal - The right to purchase a property under terms and conditions made by another purchaser and accepted by the seller. For example, if the Jones' make an offer of $120,000 on a property and the seller accepts the offer subject to the Wilson's' right of first refusal, the Wilson's have the right to buy the property for $120,000.

Return on Investment - The profit you make based on the amount you invested over a period of 1 year. Profit divided by the amount invested gives you what is known as a Cash on Cash Investment.

Sales Agreement or Sales Contract - See Agreement of Sale.

Second Mortgage - A subordinated lien, created by a mortgage loan, over the amount of a first mortgage. Second mortgages generally carry a higher rate than a first mortgage since they represent a higher risk for an investor. Mortgages are generally recorded in the order of the date they are placed.

Section 1031 - The section of the IRS code that deals with tax free exchanges of certain property. General rules for tax free exchanges are the properties must be: exchanged, similar, and used for business or as an investment.

Section 8 Housing - Privately owned rental units participating in the low-income rental assistance program. Landlords receive subsidies on behalf of qualified low-income tenants, allowing the tenants to pay a limited proportion of their incomes toward the rent.

Seller Financing - The Seller of the property agrees to hold a mortgage and accept monthly payments instead of receiving their money in one lump sum.

Sheriff's Deed - A deed given at the sheriff's sale in the foreclosure of a mortgage.

Single Family Housing (SFR) - A general term originally used to distinguish a house designed for use by one family from an apartment house. More recently, used to distinguish a house with no common area from a planned development or condominium. Example: Town houses, detached units.

Special Warranty Deed - The grantor does not warrant against title defects arising from conditions that existed before he/she owned the property. The seller warrants that he/she has done nothing to impair title.

Subject To (Purchasing subject to a mortgage) - The buyer agrees to make payments on the existing mortgage, without notifying the lender. The house is purchased "subject to the mortgage." This does not state that the buyer AGREES to pay the mortgage – it means that the property has a mortgage attached to it. The seller remains liable for making payments on the loan if the buyer does not make the mortgage payment. The buyer is not personally liable for mortgage payments, but must make payments to keep the property.

Subordination - A loan in a lower priority, for example a second mortgage is subordinate to a first.

Substitution of Liability - When assuming a mortgage, you are now liable for the loan.

Survey - Map made by a licensed surveyor who measures land and charts its boundaries, improvements and relationship to the property surrounding it.

Sweat Equity - Value added to a property due to improvements made personally by the owner.

Tax Lien - Lien for nonpayment of taxes

Tax Sale - Public sale of a property at an auction by a government authority as a result of non-payment of taxes.

Tenancy at Will - A tenancy arrangement in which one party (the tenant) occupies real estate with the permission of the owner, for an unspecified period of time. The tenant may decide to leave the property at any time or must leave at the landlords will.

Tenancy in Common - Ownership of a property by 2 or more persons, each of whom has an undivided interest, without the right of survivorship. Upon the death of one of the owners, the ownership share of the deceased is inherited by the beneficiary designated on the owner's will.

Time is of the Essence - Legal phrase in a contract requiring all references to specific dates and times noted in the contract be interpreted exactly.

Title - A legal document establishing evidence of ownership.

Title Insurance - An insurance policy which protects the insured against loss arising from a property ownership dispute. Title insurance policies are typically obtained for the buyer and the lender.

Title Report - A document indicating the current state of title. The report includes information on the current ownership, outstanding deeds of trust or mortgages, liens, easements, covenants, restrictions, and any defects.

Title Search - An examination of the public records to determine the ownership and encumbrances affecting the property.

Tract - A parcel of land generally held for subdividing.

Trust Deed - See Deed of Trust.

Trustee - A party who is given legal responsibility via a Deed of Trust to hold property in the best interest of or "for the benefit of" another. The trustee is one placed in a position of responsibility for another, a responsibility enforceable in a court of law.

Underwriting - The decision whether to make a loan to a potential home buyer based on credit, income, employment history, assets, etc.

Unencumbered Property - Real estate with free and clear title.

Unimproved Property - Land that has received no development.

VA Loan - Home loan guaranteed by the U.S. Veterans Administration, enabling a veteran to buy a home with no money down.

Valuation - An estimation of value of a property, as determined by various factors.

Variable Rate Mortgage - See Adjustable Rate Mortgage

Waiver - The voluntary renunciation, abandonment, or surrender of some claim, right, or privilege.

Warranty Deed - A deed which guarantees the title from the seller to the buyer.

Wraparound Mortgage - The seller creates a new mortgage for the buyer that includes the remaining amount on the current mortgage AND the remaining purchase price amount. The new mortgage "wraps around" the current mortgage. The seller is still responsible for the 1st mortgage. The buyer will essentially pay both mortgages (one held by the bank and one held by the seller) using one monthly payment given to the seller.

Zoning - Areas may be zoned to specify use of a property, i.e. residential, commercial, and agricultural. These zoning ordinances

www.ingramcontent.com/pod-product-compliance
Lightning Source LLC
Chambersburg PA
CBHW071423220526
45469CB00004B/1399